D1592395

a gallery of NA☒IS

edited by MORRIS CARGILL

LYLE STUART • SECAUCUS, N.J.

All photographs in this book
are the property of United Press International
and are used with their permission.

The author would like to thank Roy Mehlman
for his co-operation in the production of this book.

First Edition
Copyright © 1978 by Morris Cargill
All rights reserved, including the right to reproduce
this book or any portion thereof in any form
Published by Lyle Stuart Inc.
120 Enterprise Ave., Secaucus, N. J. 07094
Published simultaneously in Canada by George J. McLeod Limited
73 Bathurst St., Toronto, Ont.
Address queries regarding rights and permissions
to Lyle Stuart Inc.
Manufactured in the United States of America

Library of Congress Cataloging in Publication Data
Cargill, Morris.
A gallery of Nazis.
1. Nationalsozialistische Deutsche Arbeiter-Partei—
Portraits. 2. World War, 1939-1945—Atrocities—
Pictorial works. I. Title.
DD243.C37   778.9'2   77-18102
ISBN 0-8184-0256-3

INTRODUCTION

On May 7, 1945, General Alfred Jodl and Admiral Hans von Friedeburg signed on Germany's behalf the unconditional surrender which came into effect at midnight on May 8-9 and ended the European phase of World War II.

Shortly before this, in the small hours of April 29, Adolf Hitler married his mistress, Eva Braun. Immediately afterwards, he dictated his political testament—a long justification of his career in which he blamed the Jews for the German disaster, and in which he appointed Karl Doenitz as head of state and Joseph Goebbels as chancellor. On the following day, April 30, in a state of extreme nervous exhaustion, he said farewell in his bunker (from which he had not emerged since the previous January), to Goebbels, Martin Bormann and a few others. Hitler then returned to his own quarters and shot himself, while Eva Braun took poison. Their bodies were burned. So ended the Third Reich. Hitler had proclaimed that it would last for a thousand years. It had lasted a dozen.

One of Hitler's final acts was to expel Hermann Goering and Heinrich Himmler from the party. Goebbels committed suicide on May 1 and Himmler shortly thereafter. Goering, Albert Speer, Joachim von Ribbentrop and most of the other Nazi leaders were captured and tried by the Allies as war criminals at Nuremberg. Only the fate of Martin Bormann remained uncertain.

During the years in which the Third Reich existed, Hitler's Germany had, until the Russian reverses, a remarkable chain of military and political successes. Hitler showed extraordinary talents as a political leader and demagogue, and possessed an almost hypnotic power over those with whom he came in contact. The power he exercised was without precedent both in its scope and in the technical resources at his command. Yet his contributions to Germany and the world were almost wholly destructive, ending with the destruction of Germany itself.

It must be remembered, when one considers the Nazi leaders as war criminals, and the murder of millions of Jews and other people that at the beginning of Hitler's career his views were shared in whole or in part by very many men and women all over the world and by most Germans almost to the end.

By the time Germany had been defeated Hitler had reshaped the structure of nations and thus caused a new era with even greater potentialities for centralized power and for the accompanying techniques of persuasion and destruction. While Hitler lived, his techniques seemed original and distinctive. Today we see them almost everywhere that dictatorships flourish.

Of course no one man, not even a Hitler, could have brought this about singlehanded. Who were the men who helped him, who carried out his orders, who by their collective efforts were the joint architects of the Third Reich? Were they some species of monster? Or were they just ordinary people like the rest of us, caught up in a machine which they could not control?

This book is not a history of Nazism, nor does it purport to describe events in any strict chronological order. The history of Nazism, and of World War II and the years immediately preceding it, is well known. Many books have been written upon the subject. This is strictly a book of pictures, showing what the leading Nazis, and some of those who supported them, looked like. It is an attempt to reveal in victory and in defeat, the faces of the people who, in their various ways, were responsible for one of the most brutal regimes in the history of mankind.

It is, in many ways, the "ordinariness" of most of the Nazi leaders which at first strikes and then puzzles the observer. With few exceptions, they were not men of distinction or with any great talent, though they must have had organizing ability. Yet they were to harness to their purpose the talents and incredible dedication of the German people.

Part of their success in doing so, perhaps the major reason for their success, was to create a myth which had in part already been pre-sold to the German people. Hitler preached that inequality between "races" was part of a natural order, and he exalted the "Aryan race" as the primary creative element in mankind. According to Hitler the true expression of this racial factor was the *Volk*; and the state existed only to serve the *Volk*.

Accordingly, all values were determined by this measure; morality and truth depended upon whatever served the interests of the *Volk*. The Weimar Republic specifically, and democracy in general, stood condemned, for both assumed an equality between races which according to the myth did not exist; and assumed also that the best interest of the *Volk* could be decided by discussion and votes. The myth dictated that the unity of the *Volk* must be incarnated in a *Fuehrer* with absolute authority. Below the *Fuehrer* the other leaders of the movement were to be drawn from the *Volk* and were to be its safeguard.

Hitler did not, in spite of his deliberate destruction of the Weimar Republic, regard liberal democracy as his main enemy, for he believed that it was, in any event, on the verge of collapse all over the world. To him, the rival myth and appeal of Communism was his greatest enemy; not surprisingly when one considers the similarity between the idea of the incarnation of the *Volk* in one leader served by one movement, and the concept of the "dictatorship of the proletariat" embodied in one party lead by one dictator. It is often the similarities between rival ideologies, and not their differences, which provoke the greatest bitterness. In addition, Hitler was convinced that Communism was backed by international Jewry. The Jew had become, in the Nazi myth, the very incarnation of evil.

It can be said that the Nazi myth was the product of a collective lunacy with which ninety percent of the German people had become infected. But this was not the first time, or will it be the last, in which myths of one kind or another gain general acceptance. What was exceptional about Hitler's Germany was that, at one moment in time, not only had a myth found a general acceptance, but that an efficient people, potentially powerful, had also found in Hitler a demagogue capable of making all the modern techniques of communication and technology serve that myth and who also was able, by the most ruthless means, to create an entire state in its image. In the beginning was the myth, and Hitler had given it flesh and power. And the myth *was* power.

In the following pages we bring you carefully selected photographs of the most important of the men and women who served the Third Reich. It isn't practical to show all of them, or even most of them, for there were thousands. But these are the most important of those who managed to involve the world in a war and to carry out the unprecedented slaughter of millions of people in ruthlessly organized torture and murder camps.

We were subsequently to hear the excuse that the men responsible for the Nazi atrocities were simply obeying orders. The Germany of Adolf Hitler has not been the only nation in which people serving the cause of collective irrationality have pleaded in excuse of some atrocity that they were obeying orders. The uniqueness of the Nazi situation lay not in its quality but in its degree. To a degree never before equalled, myth, irrationality and cruelty became sharply focused upon one point in time; the intense concentration of a madness generally agreed upon, backed by all the technical resources of a modern state and incarnated in the absolute rule and person of one man.

New York, 1978   MORRIS CARGILL

A portrait of Adolf Hitler at the height of his power. Hitler was born on April 20, 1889, at Braunau-am-Inn on the border of Austria-Hungary. At the outbreak of the first World War in 1914, Hitler volunteered for military service and served throughout the war. He was wounded in 1916, gassed two years later, and was still hospitalized when the war ended. He was in the front line almost continuously, serving as a headquarters runner and showing great bravery in action, for which he was awarded the Iron Cross second class in December of 1914. In August 1918, he was awarded the Iron Cross first class, a rare decoration for a man with the rank of corporal. By 1933, Hitler had established himself as the absolute dictator of Germany.

1

Adolf Hitler in two characteristic poses.
He was a spellbinder as a political
orator, and achieved an almost
hypnotic dominance over the masses
of the German people.

Hitler the visionary. His eyes seemingly
fixed upon some distant goal, Hitler
is shown during the Reichstag session at
which he gave his "last warning" to
the British Empire. Seated beside
Der Fuehrer is Rudolf Hess, his chief
lieutenant. Behind is Josef Goebbels
and beside him is Baron Von Neurath.

Vienna, Austria: A huge crowd in
Heldenplatz is watching mechanized
artillery passing by in the great military
parade before Adolf Hitler on
April 7, 1938.

General Milch, Viktor Lutze and
Colonel-Lieutenant Von Doring inspect-
ing the Horst Wessel flying squadron,
named in honor of the pimp whom
Goebbels had transformed into a Nazi
martyr.

Adolf Hitler's father, Alois Hitler, born in 1837, was illegitimate, and for a time bore his mother's name, Schicklgruber. But by 1876 he had established his claim to the surname Hitler. Alois Hitler died in 1903, but left a pension and savings adequate for the support of his wife and children. His son Adolf received a secondary education, but had a poor school record and left school in 1905 at sixteen without the usual certificate.

Adolf Hitler's mother, Klara. The young Hitler overly idealized his mother. After Adolf left school he spent two idle years in Linz indulging in grandiose dreams of becoming an artist without taking any practical steps in that direction. His mother was overindulgent to him and supplied him with money. After her death in 1907, Hitler continued to draw a small allowance which she had provided for him.

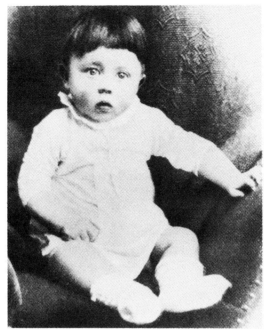

Above, Hitler is shown as a baby. Top right Hitler (under X) is shown with class comrades in his early school days. Below right, he is seen sitting with a group of comrades of the German regiment he joined in 1914, the 16th Bavarian reserve infantry ("List") regiment.

By this time Hitler was already beginning to show the traits which characterized his maturity—an inability to establish ordinary human relationships, intolerance, a hatred both of the established bourgeois world and of non-German peoples, especially Jews. He had developed a tendency to passionate outbursts and seemed to live in a world of fantasy.

A portrait of Adolf Hitler at the age of 32, taken in 1921. A year before, he had joined the tiny German Workers Party in Munich and had been in charge of the party's propaganda. In August, 1920, the German Workers Party changed its name to the National-sozialistische Deutsche Arbeiterpartei, of which Nazi became the abbreviation.

This somber-looking building at 16 Prinzregentenplatz was Hitler's house when he lived in Munich. From the time in July 1921 when Hitler became president of the Nazi party with unlimited powers, he set out to create a mass movement. The *Völkischer Beobachter* was acquired in 1920 as the party newspaper. At about this time Hitler gathered around him several of the Nazi leaders who were later to become infamous: Alfred Rosenberg, Rudolf Hess, Hermann Goering and Julius Streicher. The attempt of the party to seize power in the Munich "putsch" of November, 1923, lead to Hitler's being sentenced to prison for five years. But he served only nine months in comfort at Landsberg, and used the time to write the first volume of *Mein Kampf*.

Adolf Hitler with one of his dogs. By 1930, the Nazis became the second biggest party in Germany, winning more than six million votes in the election of that year. In the presidential elections of 1932, Hitler opposed Hindenburg and captured 36.7% of the vote.

The publisher who gave the world Hitler's *Mein Kampf*, Max Amann, former Reichleiter and S.S. Obergruppenfuehrer, who, as director of the Franzeber Publishing House, published Hitler's blueprint for world conquest. Amann is shown as he appeared before a denazification court in 1948.

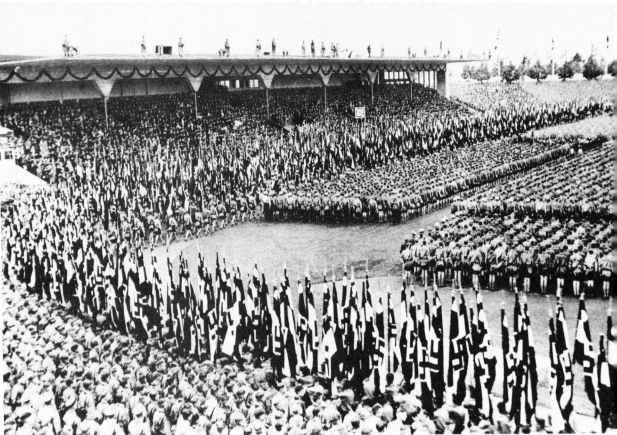

Adolf Hitler addresses crowd at
Nuremberg in 1937.

Hitlerite demonstration in Berlin in 1932.

Several thousand German boys and girls participating in a huge Nazi rally in the Neu Kollin Stadium in Berlin in 1933.

Girls for war. Young girls were also trained by the Nazis to serve the purposes of the Nazi party and of the German war machine.

This photo shows a part of the parade that marked the incorporation of the Hitler Youth (Jugend) into the Home Guard (Volkssturm) in Berlin in 1944. The Jugend members wear the dark uniform. They can also be identified by their extreme youth. They took the oath to die in the defense of the holy soil of Germany. Many of them did.

The extent to which Hitlerism was capturing the minds of the German young is revealed in this telling glimpse of little school children exchanging the Hitler salute with their teachers in Berlin in 1933.

German boys being taught by the Nazis to operate field guns. Some boys began their training as early as age six.

At the age of six German boys had to join the Nazi Youth organizations. They received strenuous physical training which left them well prepared for military service.

Adolf Hitler is driven through the streets of Nuremberg in triumph on his arrival there to attend the annual Nazi Party Congress. In 1933 Hindenburg invited Hitler to be Chancellor of Germany, and he took the office with the support of Von Papen and others.

Hitler accepting the plaudits of multitudes in Berlin. With Hitler are Hermann Goering and Paul Josef Goebbels. A fire which destroyed the Reichstag on the night of February 7, 1933, had been arranged by the Nazis but attributed to the Communists. This gave Hitler the excuse for a campaign of violence and helped to give the Nazi party 43.9% of the votes polled in the election of that year. In March the new Reichstag assembled in the Potsdam garrison church and gave Hitler full powers.

General Erich Ludendorff, Chief of Staff to Field Marshal Hindenburg at the end of World War I, gave much support to Hitler in the early days of Nazism.

25

Hitler talking to Austrian Chancellor Dr. Arthur Seyss-Inquart during the big parade that marked the annexation of Austria. Hitler justified the invasion of Austria with the official statement that he had been requested to intervene "to prevent bloodshed."

Adolf Hitler in an informal pose with the family of Nazi Propaganda Minister Paul Josef Goebbels. It was rumored that little Helmuth Goebbels (center foreground) was actually the son of Hitler and Frau Goebbels. The entire Goebbels family committed suicide in 1945.

Hitler's personal photographer, Heinrich Hoffman, still possessed an air of Nazi arrogance following his capture by 7th U.S. Army Counter Intelligence Corps near Rosenheim, Germany, on May 28, 1945. It was Hoffman who clothed and fed the Fuehrer during the early days of Nazism. He was also responsible for introducing Eva Braun to Hitler.

Hitler with the youngest daughter of Winifred Wagner, the granddaughter of composer Richard Wagner. Hitler was indifferent to clothes and food, and he never smoked or drank either coffee or tea, much less alcohol.

27

Marion Daniels, an acrobatic dancer from Chicago, who danced before Hitler. Although she claimed at one time to have been intimate with Hitler, and had flown from France in a plane sent for her by Hitler so that she could appear at Berlin's "Fastnacht" carnival celebration, it is doubtful whether there was anything more in the relationship than one of mutual admiration.

Leni Riefenstahl, one of
Germany's most talented actresses
and half-Jewish, was also reported
to have been the mistress of Adolf
Hitler. She denied this after the war.
Hitler's "great love" was Geli Raubal,
the daughter of his half-sister, Angela
Raubal. Hitler's possessive jealousy
drove Geli to suicide in September
of 1931.

Frau Gertrude Scholtz-Kling was also at one time romantically linked to Hitler by rumor. Hitler once described her as ''the perfect Nazi woman.''

The girl known as La Jana was also supposed to have been a mistress of Hitler. She became a friend of Adolf Hitler in 1937.

Unity Valkyrie Mitford, the daughter of Lord Redesdale, whose sister Diana married Sir Oswald Mosley, the leader of the British Fascists, was passionately devoted to Hitler. Finding her love unrequited, she shot herself in the head. She recovered, returned to England, and died in 1948. She is shown here being put into an ambulance on a stretcher en route to her home in Buckinghamshire, England. Other sisters in this remarkable family were novelist Nancy Mitford, writer and political radical Jessica Mitford, and Deborah, Duchess of Devonshire.

This is a photograph of "Uschi," rumored to have been the child of Hitler and Eva Braun, but probably the child of one of Eva's sisters. This photo was found among the personal belongings of Eva Braun.

Adolf Hitler and Eva Braun. Eva Braun, a shop assistant from Munich, became Hitler's mistress after she shot herself in a successful attempt to call Hitler's attention to her. Eva was a warmhearted girl of no intellectual distinction. Hitler would not consider marriage, but married Eva at the very end of their lives. 31

The surface ruins of the Berlin bunker after shelling by the Russian army. From January 1945, Hitler never left the bunker. Facing defeat, he had isolated himself more and more from reality. Martin Bormann, his secretary, saw to it that only pleasing information reached him and he became increasingly dependent upon his physician, Theodor Morell, and the injections he supplied. In a state of extreme nervous exhaustion, prematurely senile, Hitler prepared to take his own life. In the early hours of April 29, 1945, Hitler and Eva Braun were married. On April 30, Hitler said farewell to the few who remained in the bunker, then retired to his rooms with Eva where he shot himself; Eva killed herself with poison. Their bodies were burned.

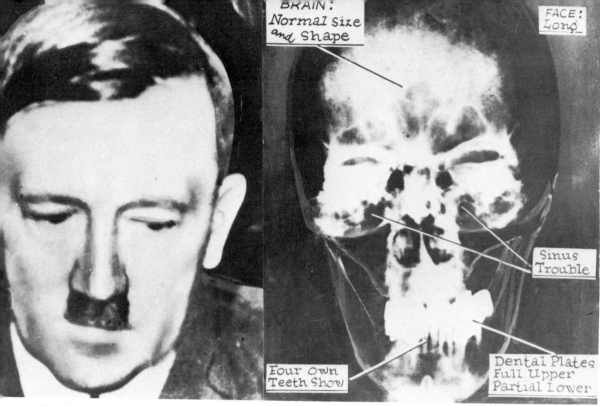

BRAIN: Normal size and Shape

FACE: Long

Sinus Trouble

Four Own Teeth Show

Dental Plates Full Upper Partial Lower

The last pictures taken of Hitler. (Left) a photo of Hitler taken shortly before his suicide. (Right) An X-ray photograph of Hitler's head taken from the file of his personal doctor. He had a "normal" brain.

Look-alike. The extraordinary resemblance to Adolf Hitler of a train conductor in Prague lead, at one time, to rumors that Hitler still lived. Photo, taken in 1945, shows Frantisek Holub, who was the same age as Hitler and had had that mustache for 30 years.

INTERLUDE

From November 20, 1945, to October 1, 1946, the
Nuremberg International Tribunal tried 24 members of
the Nazi party hierarchy as war criminals, accusing them
of "crimes against peace, war crimes and crimes
against humanity . . ." Among them three were acquitted,
twelve sentenced to death, two sentenced to 20 years,
one to 15 years and one to 10 years. Lesser leaders
were tried before various allied military tribunals.

Hermann Goering as a lieutenant in Richtofen's Flying Circus, daredevils of the German Air Force in World War I.

A portrait of an older Goering, soon after he became Field Marshal and was put in supreme command of all of Germany's air power.

January 12, 1938, during the double birthday celebration of Reichsleader Alfred Rosenberg (left) and General Hermann Goering. In Berlin at Goering's home they exchanged congratulations. Each was 45 years old. Goering had now become addicted to morphine.

Field Marshal Hermann Goering, Reich Air Minister in World War II, proudly displays his new baton during ceremonies marking the third anniversary of the creation of the new German Air Force. In his address he warned that although his air force was a weapon for peace "terrible will be the result when the command for an attack comes."

Goering arrives in Tripoli, the guest of
Marshal Italo Balbo, governor of Libya.
The Italian Guard of Honor greet him
with the Nazi salute.

Right, Hermann Goering, his country
and his air force defeated, arrives for
trial for war crimes at the Palace of
Justice at Nuremberg. He was found
guilty and sentenced to death.

Hermann Goering explains a point to an unsmiling Rudolf Hess, at their trial at Nuremberg.

Hermann Goering claps his hand over his mouth during his trial for uttering a remark out of turn, and almost gets a laugh out of Hess. On the left of Hess sits Joachim Von Ribbentrop. Behind, left to right are Karl Doenitz, Erich Raeder, Baldur Von Schirach and Fritz Sauckel.

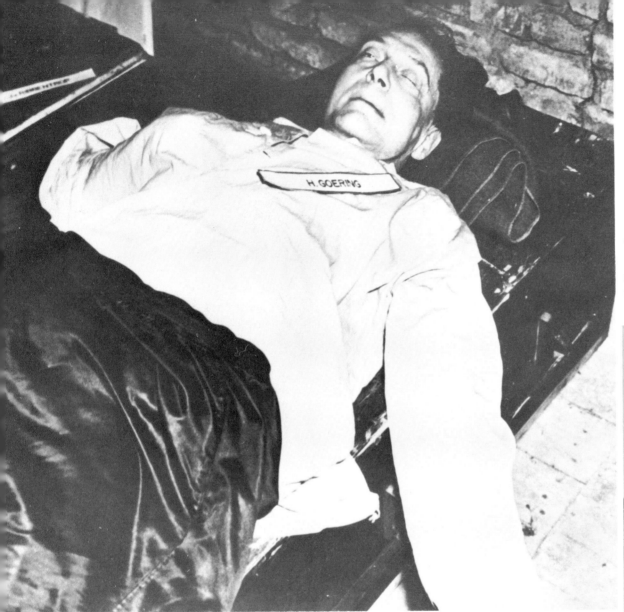

Emmy Goering goes on trial. The wife of Hermann Goering testifies on her own behalf at her trial before a denazification board in Garmisch-Partenkirchen. She was convicted, but not jailed.

The body of ex-Field Marshal Hermann Goering, who cheated the hangman by taking poison, lies on a coffin in Nuremberg Prison awaiting cremation. He was scheduled to die on the gallows on October 16, 1946, together with ten other convicted Nazi leaders, but he committed suicide at the last minute by chewing a capsule of cyanide which had been smuggled into his cell.

Another masterpiece, "Venus and Adonis," is rescued from among the loot found in Hermann Goering's treasure cave. This painting had been stolen from the Wildenstein Collection.

During World War II Hermann Goering looted millions of dollars worth of art treasures from German-occupied countries. Much of it was hidden in Goering's private treasure cave at Konigsee, near Berchtesgaden. Two American soldiers are seen displaying Vermeer's seventeenth-century masterpiece "Christ and the Adulteress" after unfolding it from the stovepipe around which it had been wrapped.

An American soldier examines a valuable work of art that rests on a wash basin.

Picture shows a small part of the loot which was recovered from Goering's

treasure cave. The loot included silver art objects and plate as well as old masters.

Ernst Roehm (left) and Rudolph Hess. In the early days of the Nazi party it was said that Hitler trusted only two men in full measure, Ernst Roehm and Rudolph Hess. On the 30th of June, 1934 (the "Night of the Long Knives"), Hitler sent a convoy of cars and armored vehicles to Wiessee and invaded the Pension Hanselbauer. With a revolver in his hand, Hitler pounded on Roehm's door, shouting, "It is I, Hitler, open the door at once!"

Roehm, a homosexual, was in bed with Count Hans Joachim Von Spreti. When Roehm unlocked the door, they were both arrested. Also arrested was Edmund Heines, police president of Breslau, who was in bed in a room opposite with a young S.A. man.

Heines and Von Spreti were almost immediately shot. But Hitler could not bring himself to have his old friend executed and told Himmler that he had pardoned Roehm because of his past services. Himmler and Goering persuaded Hitler not to pardon Roehm. Hitler then ordered Roehm be given a loaded revolver so that he could commit suicide, but Roehm refused to do so. Shortly afterwards, two S.S. men shot Roehm, who died in his cell at Stadelheim.

43

Former S.S. Nazi Col. Gen. Sepp Dietrich, left, and S.S. Col. Michael Lippert, right, two of Hitler's more accomplished gunmen are shown in the prisoner's dock in Munich where the court was probing the ''Night of the Long Knives'' of June 30, 1934, in which Hitler came to power. Dietrich and Lippert are being tried for complicity in the mass purge of brownshirts accused of planning a putsch against Hitler. Ernst Roehm's chief adjutant testified that most of his fellow brownshirt leaders executed on Hitler's orders cried out ''Long live the Fuehrer'' before being shot down by firing squads.

Wreckage of Messerschmidt plane flown by Hess. In spite of being Germany's number 3 leader under Hitler, Hess flew to Great Britain, abandoning his aircraft and bailing out over Scotland. His intention, he said, was to negotiate peace with Winston Churchill. Germany claimed he had gone mad. Hess was imprisoned in England.

Rudolf Hess, awaiting the verdict of the International Military Tribunal at Nuremberg, looking drawn and haggard. He was sentenced to life imprisonment. He is still (in 1978) serving his sentence and efforts to have him now released have been frustrated by the refusal of Russia to agree.

Rudolf Hess was brought to trial at Nuremberg after World War II. During his trial he sat most of the time staring into the distance, holding in his hands a book on German jurisprudence which he never opened. In this photo he is seen with Goering (left) and Joachim Von Ribbentrop with Karl Doenitz in the background in dark glasses.

Rudolf Hess as a child. He's with his sister, Mina.

General Alfred Jodl was condemned to death as a war criminal. Here he's seen listening to the evidence against him at his trial at Nuremberg.

Admiral Karl Doenitz, who considered
himself successor to Adolf Hitler, stands
between Reich Production Minister
Albert Speer (left) and Alfred Jodl
(right) just after their arrest at the
German High Command Headquarters
at Flensburgh.

Admiral Karl Doenitz is seen smiling
during his trial as a war criminal at
Nuremberg. He was sentenced to ten
years imprisonment.

48

Adolf Hitler and Seyss-Inquart are shown
during their meeting on February 17,
1938, when Hitler gave the newly-
appointed Austrian Minister of the
Interior his order for the Nazification
of Austria.

Seyss-Inquart in his cell during his trial
as a war criminal at Nuremberg. He
was found guilty and sentenced
to death.

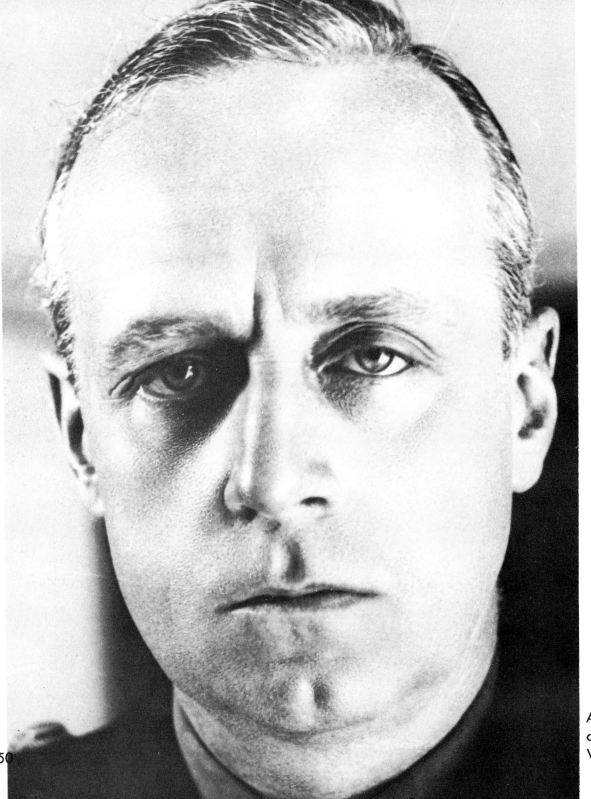

A portrait taken in the early days of the Nazi regime of Joachim Von Ribbentrop.

Herr Joachim Von Ribbentrop, German Foreign Minister, is seen with M. Georg Bonnet, French Foreign Minister, signing the "No More War" pact at the French Foreign Office in Paris. The pact was signed with gold pens on December 6, 1938.

Joachim Von Ribbentrop shown in his cell during his trial as a war criminal at Nuremberg. He was sentenced to death.

Dr. Hans Frank. While Minister of
Justice, Dr. Hans Frank maintained
private law offices where he dispensed
legal services of a favored sort and
made a fortune. He was named
Governor of Poland, and became a
brutal administrator. Of all the
defendants at Nuremberg, he was the
only one to denounce Hitler, and claimed
to be a constant reader of the Bible.
He was sentenced to death.

Field Marshal Wilhelm Keitel, who
took a prominent part in the surrender
of Germany, during his testimony at
the War Crimes Trials at Nuremberg.
He was sentenced to death.

Ernst Kaltenbruner taking the oath
before giving evidence at the Nuremberg trial in his own defense. He was
54   sentenced to death.

Admiral Raeder (left) and Walter Funk were two of the top Nazis found guilty of war crimes at Nuremberg. They were sentenced to life imprisonment.

Baron Konstantin Von Neurath was sentenced to fifteen years imprisonment at the war crimes trial in Nuremberg. Here, he is seen during his trial. He was ill and nearly blind.

Baldur Von Schirach was the first leader of the Hitler Youth Movement. He is shown (left) as he was in 1940. At right, he is shown after having served the twenty-year prison sentence imposed upon him at the Nuremberg trial.

Among other guilty men of the Nazi regime, Martin Bormann, Hitler's personal secretary, has never been found. His disappearance from Berlin has never been explained, and rumors that he escaped to various countries in Latin America have not been proved correct.

One of the many rumors was that Bormann's skull had been discovered by workmen laying a cable in a railway yard near the Berlin Wall. The skull had gold teeth of the kind Borman was said to have had. Further examination showed, however, that the skull was not Bormann's. What happened to Bormann after Germany's defeat still remains a mystery.

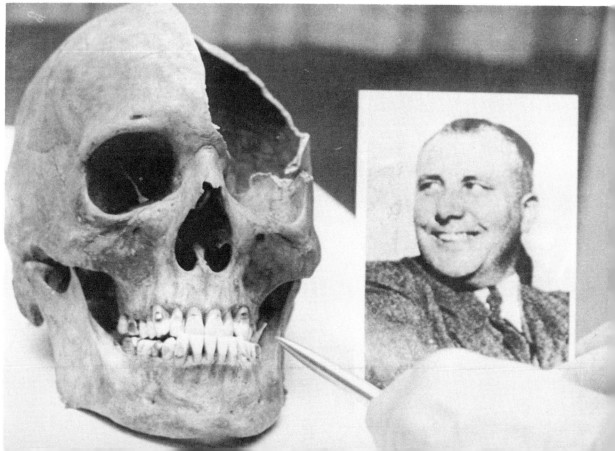

Albert Speer shows an ill-founded confidence as he inspects a sector of the Atlantic Wall in 1943. As German fear of invasion mounted, the urgency to complete the Atlantic Wall became greater, and Speer is seen urging those in charge of the building to greater efforts.

Older and wiser. Here Albert Speer and his wife, Margarethe, leave a press conference on September 30, 1966, after his release from Spandau Prison, where he served a twenty-year term as a convicted war criminal.

Fritz Sauckel (left), and Alfred Rosenberg (middle), who were sentenced to death at Nuremberg.

Wilhelm Frick standing trial at Nuremberg. He was sentenced to death.

Dr. Josef Goebbels was the notorious Reich Minister of Propaganda, who carried out Hitler's propaganda concept of the "Big Lie." At far left, an early picture of Goebbels, taken in 1931, as he leaves court after having been fined $250 for libelous writing against the German government. At left, Josef Goebbels is seen talking to General Hermann Goering, Air Minister, at a Nazi convention in Nuremberg in 1937. Below, Goebbels is shown at a street corner taking up a collection for the Nazi Party. Goebbels evaded being brought to justice by committing suicide with his wife and family.

Hans Goebbels, brother of Josef Goebbels, was a Major-General of the Nazi S.A. He is seen here after he was captured by U.S. First Army troops .

These three were acquitted at
Nuremberg. At left, Dr. Hjalmar
Schacht, Reichsbank President and
Economics Minister; (center) Franz
Von Papen, wartime ambassador to
Turkey and (right) Hans Fritsche, one-
time Nazi press chief. These three were
released from their prison cells an
hour after the court returned its verdict.

Baron Von Neurath (right) and Konrad
Heinlein (wearing glasses) pictured
here as they and other Nazi officials
listened to Adolf Hitler's speech at the
Tenth Nazi Party Congress at
Nuremberg in September 1938. The
demands made by Hitler in his speech
were granted by the British and French
without the consent of Czechoslovakia.
Konrad Heinlein was known as the
Hitler of Czechoslovakia.

Left to right: Lieutenant Wagner,
Lieutenant Pernel, Lieutenant Brueckner,
Captain Roehm after sentence of one
year for participation in the famous
"Beer Hall" putsch of 1923.

Horst Wessel, a young Berlin S.A. leader who was killed in 1930, during the campaign for the elections on the 14th of September of that year. Horst Wessel was a pimp, who had written a popular Nazi marching song. His death had nothing to do with politics; it came about during an argument over a whore. Nonetheless, Dr. Goebbels turned him into a Nazi martyr.

Horst Wessel's funeral. Hitler and his followers attended the unveiling of the tombstone over the grave of Horst Wessel in 1933. Next to Hitler is Josef Goebbels.

After the fall of France, Hitler rewarded twelve of his generals by promoting them to Field Marshal. One of them was General Milch of the German Air Force, shown here talking with Charles A. Lindbergh (left) in 1937 at the annual meeting of the Lilienthal Society for Air Transport Research held in Munich. Lindbergh flew his own plane from London to attend the meeting.

General Milch (second from right),
at that time German Undersecretary
for Air, is shown with his party upon
arrival in Rome in 1936 for a
conference with Mussolini.

Field Marshal Albert Von Kesselring, shown at the Berchtesgaden Hof, after surrendering to Maj. General Maxwell Taylor, of the 101st Airborne Division, U.S. Seventh Army, May 1945.

Sepp Dietrich, the Bavarian S.S. Gruppenfuehrer, who was later to become General of a Panzer Army, was appointed by Himmler in 1933 as head of 120 carefully chosen S.S. men called the Adolf Hitler Bodyguard.

Gregor Strasser, one-time close confidante of Chancellor Adolf Hitler and a power in his Nazi organization, who was shot by Heydrich on June 30, 1934, along with Gen. Kurt Von Schleicher and many other Nazis who had incurred the enmity of Himmler or Heydrich.

In May 1933, the German trade unions were dissolved with the aid of the stormtroopers and were replaced by the German Labor Front. Including employers as well as employees, capital as well as labor, the Labor Front was a branch of the Nazi Party. Robert Ley, above, was appointed its leader.

Joseph Buerkel, to whom Hitler delegated the task of reorganizing the Austrian National Socialist Party. It was he whom Hitler chose to run the Saar area when it was taken over in 1934. He was one of the most militant of the Nazis, and was a leader of the anti-Catholic movement.

General Franz Ritter Von Epp, who was a founder of the Freikorps which crushed the Berlin and Munich Soviets in 1919, became one of Hitler's secret supporters in the early days of Nazism.

Otto Abetz, Hitler's Ambassador to France.

Dr. Anton Rintelen, the Austrian diplomat, was arrested as chief of the Austrian Nazis and sentenced to 20 years imprisonment following the assassination of the chancellor of Austria, Dr. Engelbert Dollfuss. Dr. Rintelen is pictured here in his home with his daughter Anne Marie, following his release from prison under the amnesty forced on Austria by Adolf Hitler in his "Nazification" of that nation. Three thousand other political prisoners were released at the same time.

Arthur Greiser. Known as the hangman of the Poles, Greiser, the chief Nazi official in the Poznan district of Poland was one of the most detested of all Nazis. His reign in Poland was marked by one bloody atrocity after another, the worst being the mass shooting of 100 Polish political prisoners in 1942 for the killing of two Gestapo men by a Polish army sergeant.

German industrialist Fritz Thyssen, who helped finance Hitler's rise to power in Germany, fled Germany with his family after the war, blaming the Nazis for having started it. He went to Switzerland, then to France, ending up in Buenos Aires, Argentina, where, on February 8, 1951, he died in his sleep at the age of 78. He is seen here with his wife and their son-in-law, Count Zichy. Seated (left to right) are Countess Zichy, Thyssen's only daughter, and their son Fritz August.

Germany's tobacco king, Philip Reemtsma, leaves court in Hamburg where he was charged with bribing Hermann Goering to the extent of a million marks yearly. Reemtsma was one of the wealthiest industrialists of prewar Germany, and he was an enthusiastic supporter of the Nazis at one time.

Charged for buying women. Christian Schneider, former chief of the Central Personnel department of I. G. Farben is shown in the dock at the Nuremberg Tribunal where he and other Farben officials were tried for war crimes. A witness testified that the Farben combine purchased 150 women from the concentration camp at Oswicim for use as guinea pigs in testing a new drug. All the women died during the tests.

Alfred Krupp on trial at Nuremberg.
The great German munitions king
(center), sole owner of the giant Krupp
munitions combine, sits and hears
testimony concerning his treatment of
slave laborers. Krupp was forced to
sit side by side with his former financial
director, Ewald Loeser (right). Loeser
left Krupp in 1943 as a result of bitter
personal enmity.

Nuremberg, 1947. Here are four of the top officials of I. G. Farben, the great German chemical trust, who were indicted by the United States on charges of fomenting and waging aggressive war, mass murder, plunder and spoliation. Cartel agreements between I. G. Farben and American companies prevented the U.S. from shipping essential war materials to Britain and other allies until the U.S. entered the war. The accused above are Herman Schmitz, chairman of the I. G. Farben board and director of the Bank for International Settlements; George Von Schnitzler, director of home and foreign sales and military economy chief; Karl Krauch, Goering's special advisor on chemical production, and Heinrich Hoerlein, chief of chemical research.

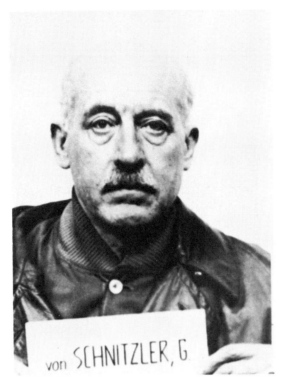

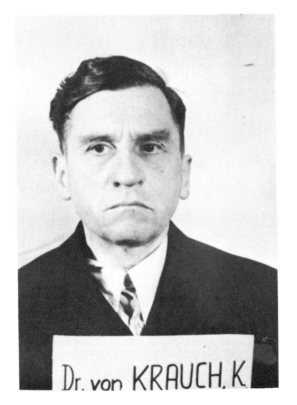

Nuremberg. The trial of six of those accused of helping to build the Nazi war machine. Seated in the prisoner's box during a court recess, they are (left to right) Karl Krauch, Herman Schmitz, Max Ilgner, George Von Schnitzler, Fritz Gajewski and Heinrich Gattineau.

Adolf Eichmann also escaped after Germany's defeat, but was captured in Buenos Aires, Argentina, by Israeli agents in April 1960. Eichmann was taken to Israel and tried as a war criminal.

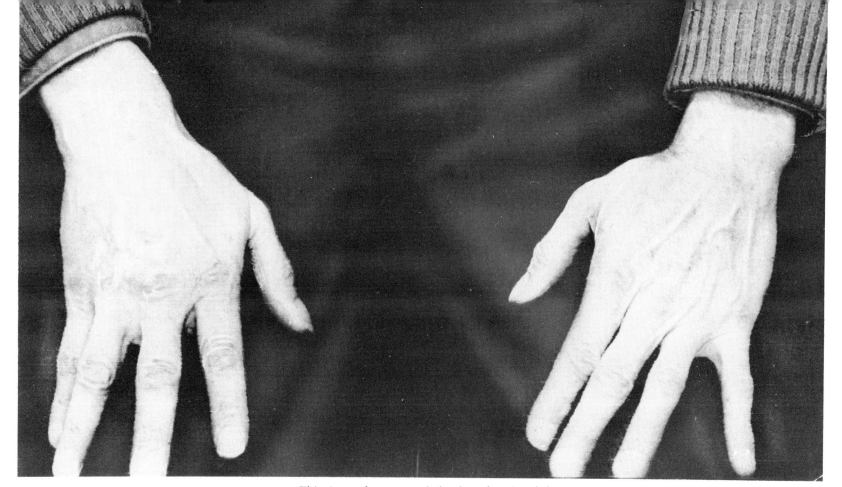

This is a close-up of the hands of Adolf Eichmann, hands that ordered the destruction of millions of Jews. In his defense, Eichmann claimed that he was only obeying orders from his Gestapo boss, Heinrich Mueller. The Israeli court sentenced him to death by hanging.

Frau Adolf Eichmann, wife of the executed war criminal demonstrates to the press in Munich how she said good-bye to her husband in jail in Israel before his execution. They placed their hands together, but were separated by a glass partition.

Horst Eichmann and his three brothers lived in the house where his father was captured. Horst was twenty years old in 1960 and was Eichmann's second son. Young Eichmann, wearing an olive shirt, boots and a swastika armband is shown at a press conference in Buenos Aires, Argentina, in 1964. He was observing the anniversary of his father's execution, and referred to his father as a "martyr who devoted his whole life to the struggle for a freer and more just Fatherland."

Aides of Eichmann. Nazi S.S. officers Herman Krumey (left) and Otto Hunsche were sentenced at a Frankfurt Court in August 1969 for aiding the murder of at least 300,000 Hungarian Jews. Krumey drew a life sentence and Hunsche was sentenced to 12 years.

Heinrich Himmler. In 1927 Himmler became deputy leader of the S.S. Blackshirts and was appointed leader in 1929. As deputy head of the Reich administration in 1939 he was empowered by Hitler to suppress anti-Nazi resistance. By 1944 Himmler, as chief of Gestapo, had assumed administrative control of Germany, replacing Hermann Goering as the Nazi second-in-command. A fanatical Nazi, Himmler was responsible for the death of several million people.

Suicide of Himmler. The identity papers which Himmler carried with him gave him the new name of Hitzinger which aroused the suspicions of British soldiers at Bremervoerde where they arrested Himmler on May 21, 1945. On May 23, however, the Gestapo chief was able to swallow the contents of a vial of cyanide and died within a few minutes. Shown here is the small empty vial recovered from his body.

Frau Heinrich Himmler. The wife of the Gestapo head.

Julius Streicher, the Nazi director in charge of the extermination of Jews, was sentenced to death by the International Military Tribunal in Nuremberg. Photo at left, shows Streicher as he appeared at a Nazi party rally in Berlin in 1934, clearly revealing his brutal nature. Photo at right presents a different appearance as Streicher is tried in 1946 at the Palace of Justice.

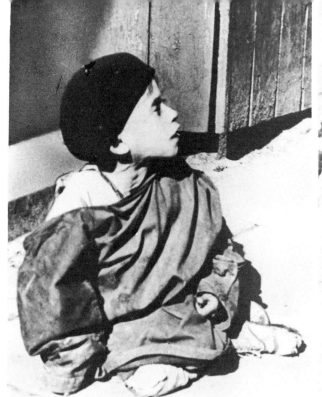

Poland. Photo of pitifully undernourished
Jewish children were found among
others in Streicher's files.

The despair of starvation, the utter
hopelessness etched deeply across the
face of this Jewish child. Photo was
found in Streicher's files.

The Beast of Belsen. S.S. Hauptsturm-
fuehrer Josef Kramer commanded the
Belsen camp. British Second Army forces
upon arrival at Belsen found about
60,000 civilians dying from typhus,
typhoid or dysentery, and hundreds of
dead littering the grounds.

Grese and Kramer. Another picture of
Josef Kramer, known as the Beast of
Belsen. He is shown with Irma Grese,
brutal woman commandant of the death
camp. They are shown awaiting trial
as war criminals in the yard of the
prison at Celle.

The Nazi who confessed. Rudolph Hoess, formerly the boss of Josef Kramer, the Beast of Belsen, confessed that he supervised the death by poison gas of about two million prisoners. On his arrest by British authorities he said, "I built Auschwitz from a small collection of huts into the greatest murder camp the world has ever known."

Nuremberg. In the courtroom where top-ranking officials of the Nazi hierarchy were tried before an allied tribunal, twenty-three German doctors stand up for the entrance of the judges during their arraignment in November 1946 on charges of murdering thousands of concentration camp inmates in medical experiments. Standing behind the double row of the accused are the American guards. The defendants are (left to right) Gerhard Rose, Siegfried Ruff, Victor Brack, Hans Wolfram Fomberg, Herman Becker-Freyseng, George August Weltz, Konrad Schaefer, Waldemar Hoven, Wilhelm Beiglbosk, Adolf Pokorny, Herta Oberhauser, (the only woman doctor) and Fritz Fischer. Front row (left to right) Karl Brandt, Siegfried Handloser, Paul Rostock, Oskar Schroeder, Karl Genzken, Karl Gebhart, Kurt Blome, Joachim Mrugowsky, Rudolf Brant, Helmut Poppendick, and Wolfram Sievers.

Hitler's doctor, Dr. Karl Brandt, is condemned to death by hanging at Nuremberg. Hitler's personal physician spent much time experimenting upon prisoners in concentration camps. Most of the experiments were inhuman and caused long and agonizing death to his victims.

Dr. Hans Hefelmann faces the court at
Limburg, Germany, on trial for the
"mercy killing" of 100,000 handicapped
Germans. Three former colleagues were
also to have been tried with him—
Werner Heyde, Friedrich Tillman and
Bernhard Bohne. But the first two com-
mitted suicide while the third fled to
Argentina.

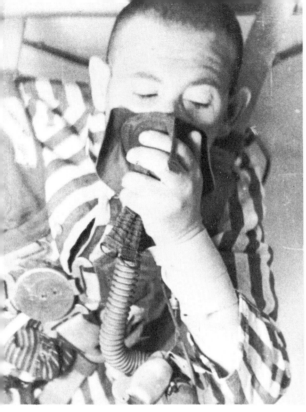

The following photos were made by German doctors of an experiment in compression and decompression which they carried out on an inmate of a concentration camp. At the end of the experiment the "human guinea pig" is dead of "the bends."

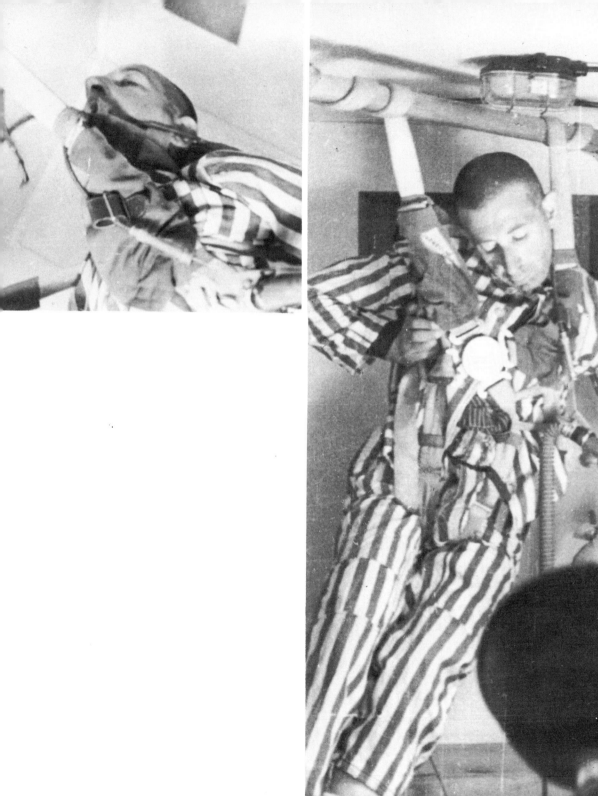
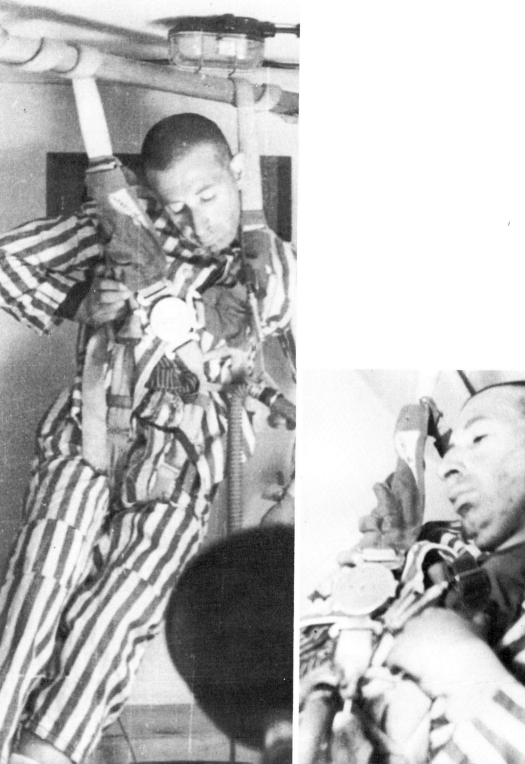

"The Angel of Death." Dr. Joseph Mengele, the former medical officer at Auschwitz concentration camp who is still uncaptured and somewhere in South America, if he is still alive. Mengele, who was called "the Angel of Death," held two degrees, an M.D. and a Ph.D. He performed thousands of experiments on children, trying to make perfect Aryans—to change brown eyes into blue eyes with chemicals and through genetic experiments. He's shown above as a young man.

This picture of Dr. Mengele, taken in 1960, when he was arrested in Peru, though subsequently released. During World War II, Dr. Mengele was responsible for thousands of deaths. He murdered twins, adults as well as children, using the subjects for biological experiments on genetic mutations.

Dr. Ernst Illing, charged with the "mercy" killing of 250 ill or defective children, is seen telling the court that he saw nothing wrong with his conduct since it was approved by Adolf Hitler.

In the first mass atrocity trial within the American occupation zone in Wiesbaden, Germany, there were six German male defendants and one female. They were charged with the murder of 500 Polish and Russian slave laborers killed at a mental institution. Lethal injections of morphine and scopolamine were used. The lone feminine defendant, Irmgard Huber, chief nurse at the institution, and Alfons Klein, executive head of the place are pictured conferring with their counsel at their trial.

Nazi doctor Werner Heyde, who committed suicide in his cell by hanging himself. He was to have been chief defendant at a trial in Limburg, Germany, for his involvement in Nazi extermination camps.

Belsen atrocities. Among twelve persons tried at Luenberg, for atrocities committed at Belsen concentration camp were Fritz Klein (left) the camp doctor who helped select victims for the gas chamber and (right) one of the Belsen guards, Peter Weingarten.

The trial began in February 1961, of Karl Chmielewski for mass murder, at Ansbach, Germany. The former S.S. officer turned sculptor after the war was once commandant of the Gusen concentration camp. He was charged with freezing to death about 100 inmates of the camp by spraying water on them in freezing weather. He is charged with the murder of 297 persons, having caused the deaths of numerous other Jewish inmates by other means.

Three more former Nazi officials of the
perfidious Auschwitz concentration
camp. Left to right, Oswald Kaduk,
Dr. Viktor Capesius and Emil Bedenark.

Architects of death. Walter DeJaco (left) and Fritz Ertl constructed the gas chambers of Auschwitz concentration camp in which at least two million Jews were exterminated. Murder charges were also brought against them.

Dr. Horst Fischer. The East German
Supreme Court led by judge Dr. Heinrich
Toeflitz sentenced Dr. Fischer to death,
for having selected at least 70,000
inmates of Auschwitz for the gas
chamber.

Erich Rajaowitsch, who called himself
Enrico Raja (left) beside a guard
as his trial begins in Vienna. His offense
was having deported 8,000 Dutch Jews
to the gas chambers of Auschwitz in
1941.

Wilhelm Bork. Like other war criminals, Bork awaits trial in the former horror camp at Dachau. He was responsible for killing five Allied fliers who parachuted down over Germany.

Wilhelm Friedrich Ruppert, one of the top men at Dachau. He is shown awaiting trial, imprisoned in the same cells at Dachau in which he kept his prisoners. The book he is reading is a German translation of *Gone With the Wind*.

Alex Bernard Hans Pickowski (right)
the former commandant of Dachau, the
most horrible of the Nazi concentration
camps, is shown after his capture by
British troops.

Engelbert Nirdermayer (right) who was in charge of the notorious crematorium at Dachau is shown with his cellmate, an S.S. Trooper who was also wanted as a war criminal.

Captured in Brazil, Franz Stangl (right) is accompanied by a police officer as he is taken by car to an aircraft bound for Germany. Stangl had hidden out in Brazil after World War II and was discovered there by Simon Wiesenthal, head of the Jewish Documentation Center in Vienna. He was returned to Germany in June 1967 for trial for war crimes. Stangl was the former commander of the Nazi extermination camps at Solidor and Treblinka.

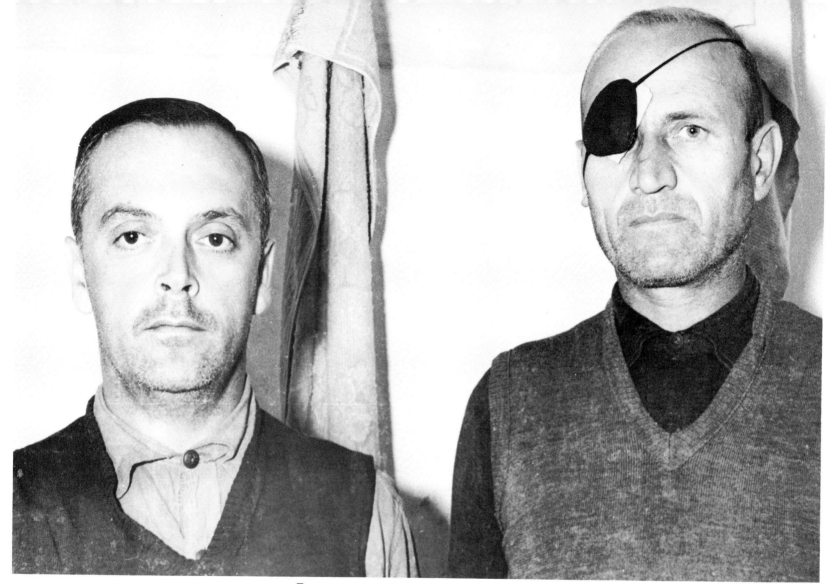

Two concentration camp commandants, Arthur Liebehenschel (left) and Otto Foerschner (right) are shown in their cell at Dachau after capture.

Karl Hermann Frank. He was held
personally responsible for the destruction
of Lidice and the murder of thousands
of Czechs following the assassination
of Reinhard Heydrich. Here, Frank
stands before a crucifix in the people's
court in Prague. Born a Czech, he
collaborated with the Germans in
advance of Hitler's march into that
country. He was appointed Minister of
State during the Nazi occupation.

Belsen women. In Nazi Germany, women equalled the bestiality and brutality of the men. Picture shows S.S. women guards at the Belsen concentration camp. Some of these husky, well-fed women were forced by the British to help bury some of the thousands of their victims.

109

A close-up of some of the vicious
Belsen S.S. women guards.

Belsen S.S. women on trial. Here are some of the Nazi women war criminals on trial for their lives as they sit in the dock during a session of their trial at Luenberg. Some of the most notorious of the Belsen officials were Herta Ehlert (8), Irma Grese (9), Ilse Litre (10) and Hilde Lobauer (11).

Close-up of Hilde Lobauer. She was described as the "S.S. woman without a uniform." Originally a political prisoner at Belsen, Hilde was promoted to internee in charge of one of the camps and soon showed a marked streak of cruelty and viciousness. Sent to Auschwitz, she helped the infamous Dr. Klein to pick out victims for gas experiments.

Irma Grese sullenly poses outside jail. She was the chief of the brutal women guards. She is wearing heavy army boots by choice.

Theodora Binz, the woman who taught Irma Grese how to commit the atrocities that eventually resulted in her death on the scaffold. Binz joined the S.S. as a teenager and worked her way up to the position of chief woman S.S. guard at Ravensbruck camp. She trained the women guards for all the concentration camps.

Dr. Herta Oberhauser, the only woman doctor among the numerous Nazi physicians tried for war crimes at Nuremberg. Here she stands beside an American military policeman and hears herself sentenced to twenty years for brutal experiments on concentration camp inmates.

Mass murder of the mentally ill. Dr. Hilde Wornicke and smiling nurse Helene Winczorek were sentenced to death by a German court for the murder of hundreds of insane patients at Obrawalde sanitorium in 1943 and 1944.

Stella Isaaksohn, alias Stella Kuebler,
a young Jewish woman who betrayed
hundreds of fellow Jews to the Gestapo.

Ilse Koch, red-haired widow of a former
commandant of the Buchenwald
concentration camp, hears herself
sentenced to life imprisonment
by a U.S. war crimes court at Dachau.
Frau Koch was pregnant with a baby
conceived in prison. Koch was notorious
for her manufacture of lampshades
and other articles made from human skin.

Above, Bishop G. Bromney Oxnam of
New York, studies samples of tattooed
and tanned human skin found in the
home of Ilse Koch.
Top right, more samples of tattooed
human skin.
At right, future U. S. Senator Thomas
Dodd holds a shrunken human head.

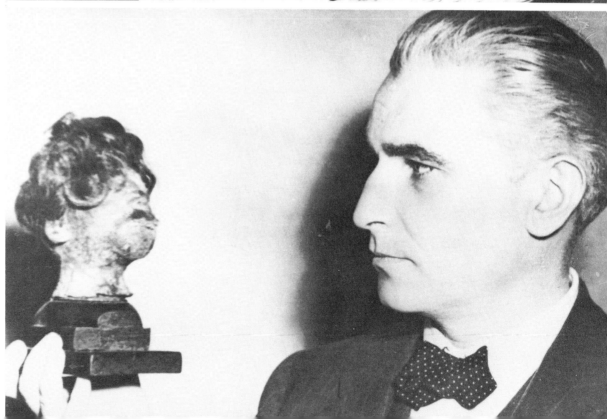

Oswald Pohl, former S.S. general who carried out the destruction of the Warsaw ghetto in which 56,000 Polish Jews were exterminated. Pohl was also in charge of the administration of all concentration camps. He was sentenced to death.

A sorry looking specimen is Captain Bakos, former member of the Hungarian S.S. He is shown awaiting trial in Salzburg in 1946 for his part in the shooting of five captured American airmen. Bakos was stripped of his necktie and shoelaces to prevent him from committing suicide.

A trio of Hungarian war criminals. Left to right, Ladislas Endre, who was the chief executioner of Jews in Hungary during the German occupation; Ferenc Zzalasi, who was "Fuehrer" of the Hungarian Nazis; and Bela Imredy, the former Hungarian Prime Minister. They were arrested by U.S. Forces in Austria and are shown as they arrived in Budapest for trial.

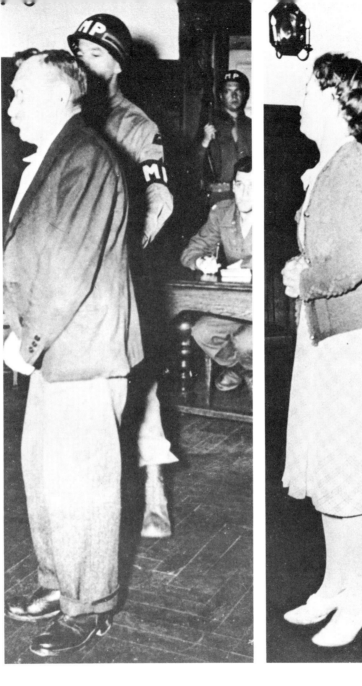

All for death. Left to right, Johann Opper; a blank stare was his only reaction on hearing the death sentence. Kathe Reinhardt found guilty of murder and sentenced to death opened her mouth to say something, then she staggered away speechless with the guard. Josef Hartgen, his face expressionless even after hearing the death sentence; and Philip Guttlich who was also hanged. These four were among the ten Germans found guilty of having taken part in the slaying of six American airmen in Russelsheim in August 1944. Seven were sentenced to death and three to long terms of imprisonment.

Butcher of Warsaw caught in Japan. Acting on a tip given them by the Tokyo police, Clark Lee, of International News Service and two other war correspondents discovered the Japanese hideaway of Gestapo Col. Josef Albert Meisinger, and convinced the high ranking war criminal to surrender to them. Known as the Butcher of Warsaw, Meisinger was charged with the murder of more than 100,000 Warsaw Jews. Here, the "Butcher" is being turned over by the newsmen to the U.S. Army Counter-intelligence Corps in Yokohama, Japan.

Royal Sadist. Prince Josiah Zu Waldeck, the first member of the German royalty to be tried for war crimes. He is shown before the court at Dachau and was tried by a U.S. Military Tribunal representing the United Nations.

Kurt Daluege, S.S. General and former Reichsprotector for Bohemia and Moravia was sentenced to hang by an extraordinary people's court in Prague on October 23, 1946. Daluege was sentenced for war crimes against Czechoslovakia. He was the first war criminal to be sentenced according to the Nuremberg decision, which declared the S.S. and leadership of the Nazi Party criminal organizations.

Here is Daluege but a few moments before execution. Dr. Kozak, President of the Court reads the death sentence. Executioners in black wait in the background to take him to the gallows.

Charged with murder. Former members of the first S.S. Panzer Regiment, these young men are shown during their trial at Dachau. They were being tried for their part in the massacre of American prisoners of war during the historic Battle of the Bulge. Scores of American soldiers, caught in the first surge of the German counter-offensive, were shot down in cold blood at Malmedy. These men confessed to going through the field of fallen American soldiers and finishing off those wounded by shooting them in the head.

Earphones on head to listen to judge's
pronouncement, top Nazi Gottlob
Berger remains impassive as he hears
himself sentenced to twenty-five years
in prison for participation in Nazi war
crimes. He was one of a long series
of defendants upon whom judgment
was pronounced by the court at
Nuremberg after long drawn-out trials.

Murderers of Anne Frank. Three Nazis, convicted of sending fifteen-year-old Anne Frank and 83,000 other Jews to their deaths during World War II, stand with their guards on February 24, 1967, as they are sentenced to prison terms. Gertrud Slottke (left), 64, received a five-year sentence; Wilhelm Zeepf (center), 58, was given a nine-year term; and Dr. Wilhelm Harster (right), 62, was sentenced to fifteen years imprisonment.

Vidkun Quisling, Norway's arch traitor—
his name was the source of a new word.
Quisling is shown arriving at his place
of trial. He was sentenced to death and
was shot October 24, 1945.

Called one of the bloodiest Nazi murderers in Hungary, Andras Kun, an excommunicated monk, is shown before the court as he listened to the testimony of a woman who witnessed one of his crimes. This woman saw Kun and his band slaughter 94 Jews on the bank of the blue Danube. On a freezing winter night he ordered the 94 to remove their clothing. He then ordered his men to fire on the helpless group. Those who were alive after the shooting were thrown into the icy river. Andras Kun and his band killed 580 Jews in November and December of 1944. Kun was sentenced to death and he was hanged two hours after the sentence was pronounced.

INTERLUDE

By as early as 1933, the first Nazi concentration camps had already been organized. The first, under Goering's charge, was at Oranienburg, near Berlin. The second, under Himmler's jurisdiction was at Dachau in Bavaria.

The first prisoners were Socialist and Communist deputies in the Reichstag. About four thousand alleged Communists were arrested after the Reichstag fire together with an assortment of Catholics, Jews and Social Democrats.

Terrorism and torture became the official policy of the Nazis. When the officials of the Ministry of Justice protested against the disregard of proper prison routine, they were ignored. At one time, moderates in the Nazi Party protested to Hitler against the cruelty and torture in the prisons. Hitler flew into a rage, literally frothing at the mouth, and shouted at them:

"Why babble about brutality and be indignant about torture? The masses want that. They need something that will give them a thrill of horror. I forbid you to change anything. By all means punish one or two men so that the German Nationalist donkeys may sleep easy. But I don't want the concentration camps changed into penitentiary institutions. Terror is the most effective political instrument. I shall not permit myself to be robbed of it simply because a lot of bourgeois mollycoddlers choose to be offended by it. People will think twice about opposing us when they hear what to expect in the camps. It's your business to see that no evidence about such cases leaks out. I cannot allow such absurd trifles to break in on my work. Anybody who is such a poltroon, that he cannot bear the thought of someone nearby having to suffer pain had better join a sewing circle, but not my party comrades."

Main entrance to Dachau Prison in Germany.

133

Scattered about the train yards of Dachau camp were bodies of prisoners who died in boxcars en route to other camps.

G.I.'s silently inspect some of the railroad
cars loaded with dead. These cars
were found on rail sidings, abandoned,
at the Dachau camp.

Dachau Internment camp. Prisoners at Dachau flirt with girls in women's ward through straw fence around same.

Women's ward used to be used as a brothel for preferred prisoners.

Dachau Internment Camp: Prisoners look
out from barbed wire fence around
camp to cheer liberating U.S. forces.

More Dachau camp survivors line the
electric fence to cheer the American
forces that liberated them.

German civilians had been escorted by
American military police from Weimar to
the concentration camp at Buchenwald.
Here they are lined up at a yard in
the camp to see a camp prisoner as he
was left hanging by the Germans.

British members of Parliament, including
Mrs. Mavis Tate, viewing their most
gruesome sight—a pile of bodies
of men who had died within the
past 24 hours at Buchenwald.

At Buchenwald, Congresswoman Claire Booth Luce talks with an emaciated eighteen-year-old Czech prisoner who was being treated in the prison camp hospital which was formerly used as the camp's brothel.

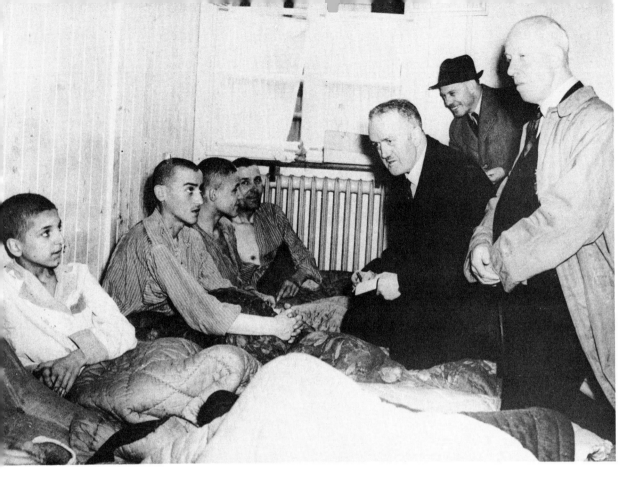

Sir Henry Morris Jones and Sir Grahame
White visit patients in the Buchenwald
hospital, formerly the camp brothel,
and take notes on their experiences.

A truckload of bodies of prisoners of the Nazis in Buchenwald. The bodies were about to be disposed of by burning when the camp was captured by Allied troops.

Bodies at the horror camp known as Buchenwald.

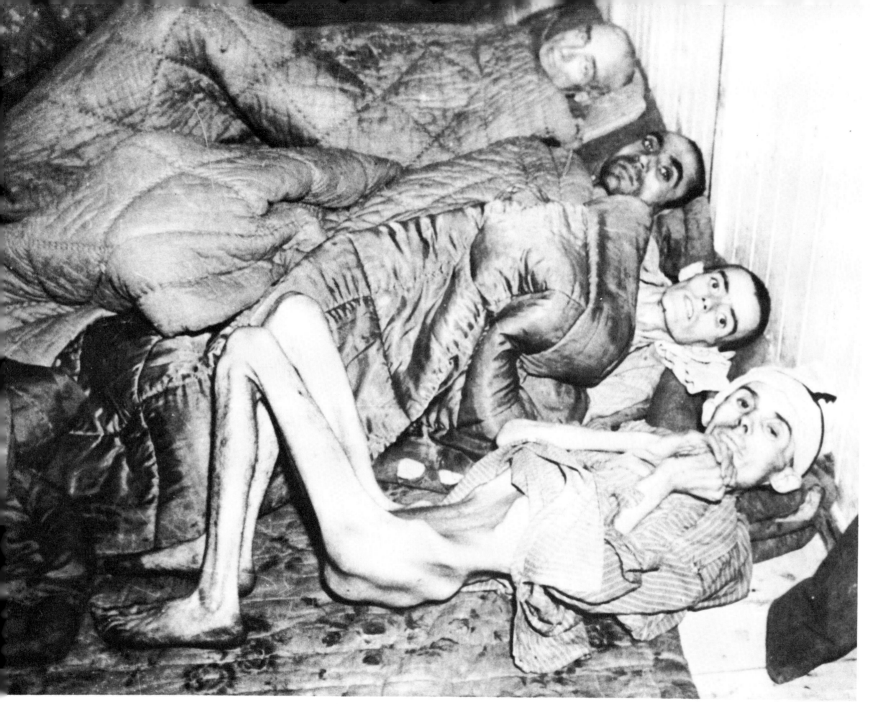

Inmates of the Buchenwald concentration
camp near Weimar, Germany.

Buchenwald concentration camp. Here, two women make the best of a tin of water for washing.

146

Russian slave laborer among Buchenwald
prisoners liberated by U.S. Third
Armored Division, Third U.S. Army,
points out one former Nazi guard who
brutally beat prisoners.

Pictured in the notice board erected at the entrance to Belsen concentration camp with its graphic description for the whole world to read.

Dr. Klein, a Storm Troop doctor, reported to have committed to death thousands of women, men and children in the Belsen camp is shown as he spoke before a microphone for British newsreels after his capture.

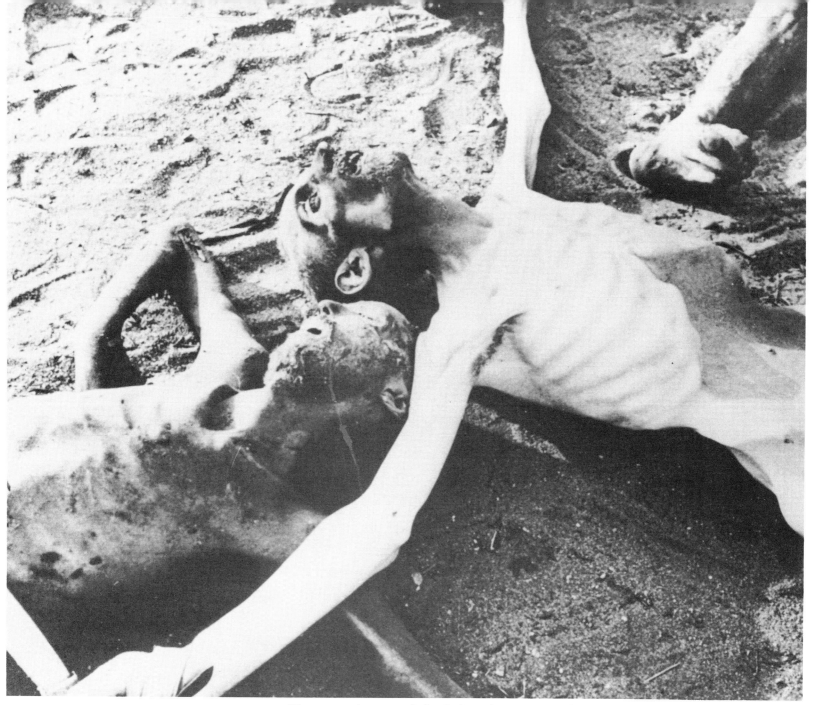

The ground area of the Belsen horror camp was littered with these starved bodies, when the British entered. Most of the 60,000 inmates were either dead or dying of starvation and brutal treatment.

A British soldier listens in horror to the ghastly story told to him by Louis Bonerquer, a starving Londoner, who is still wearing his striped prison rags.

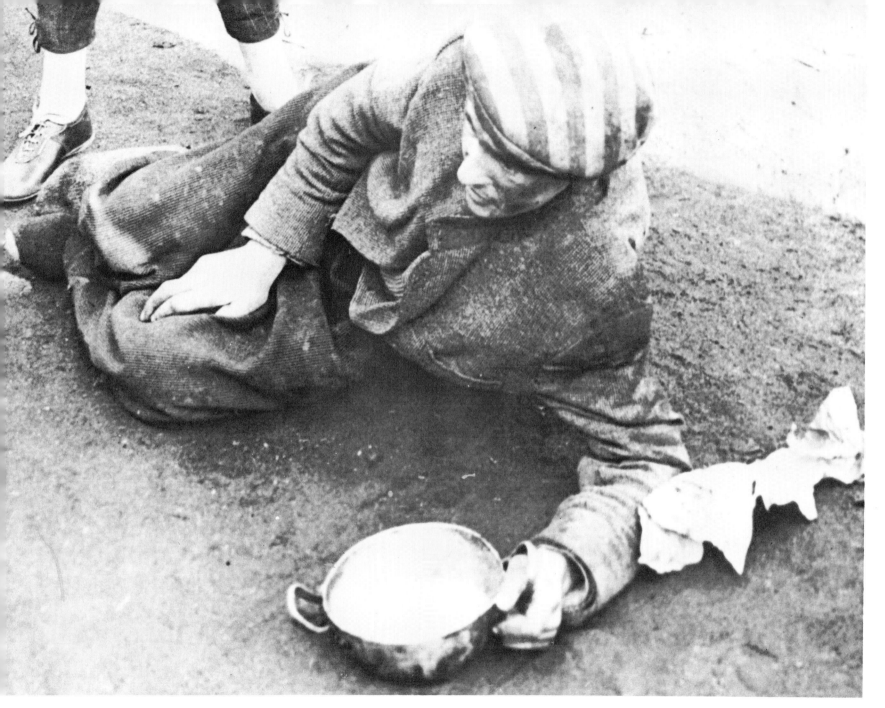

At Belsen horror camp, a man too weak to stand and almost too weak to drink the soup which has been brought to him, after the camp's liberation.

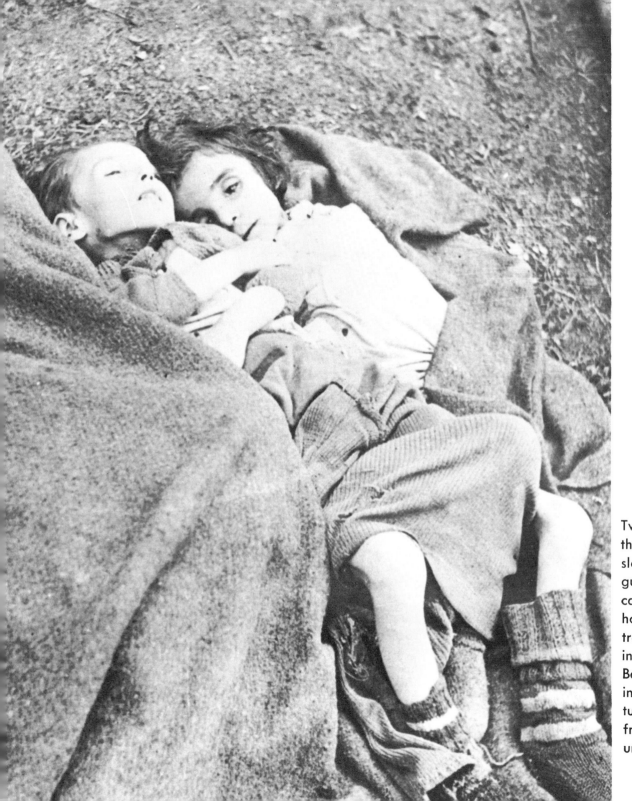

Two little children who were among the thousands of civilians forced to die a slow death by starvation by their Nazi guards at the infamous Belsen death camp. They were one of the first horrifying discoveries made by British troops when they entered the camp during the advance through Germany. Besides the thousands of corpses found in the camp, hundreds of other unfortunate victims died hourly despite the frantic efforts made by British medical units to save them.

Some of the dead at Belsen concentration camp.

A seemingly endless pile of bodies at
Belsen horror camp.

At Belsen, a living skeleton is seen
attempting to delouse his clothes.

Some of the Belsen camp inmates are
sprayed with an insecticide after allied
troops had liberated them.

At Belsen, the boots of the dead are
piled up to be used for fuel.

One of the pitiful civilian prisoners, his face scarred and swollen from beatings, is about to take a drink of water, his first in six days, from a rusty tin can. This photo was taken shortly after the arrival of British 2nd Army units.

S.S. guards loading trucks with bodies of their victims for transport to the burial grounds. In background, British soldiers stand on guard with rifles, horror and disgust on their faces.

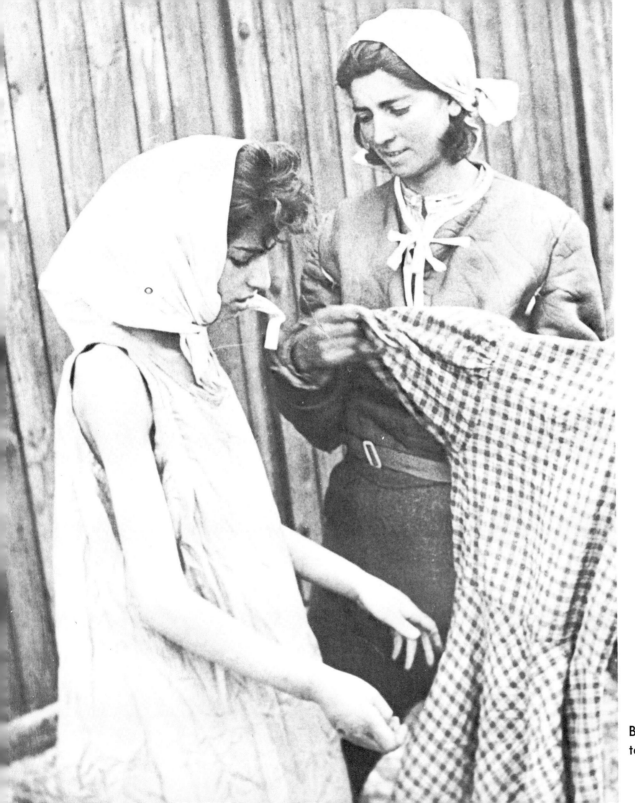

Belsen horror camp. This girl, too weak to dress, is helped by a friend.

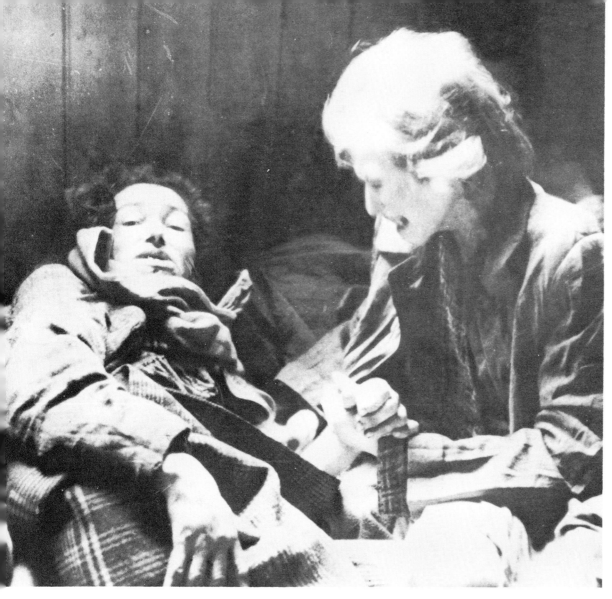

Photo shows women dying in the
so-called hospital of the camp.

163

A communal grave at Belsen.

Starved and emaciated, these two women inmates at Belsen are too weak to show much emotion after the liberation of the camp in April, 1945.

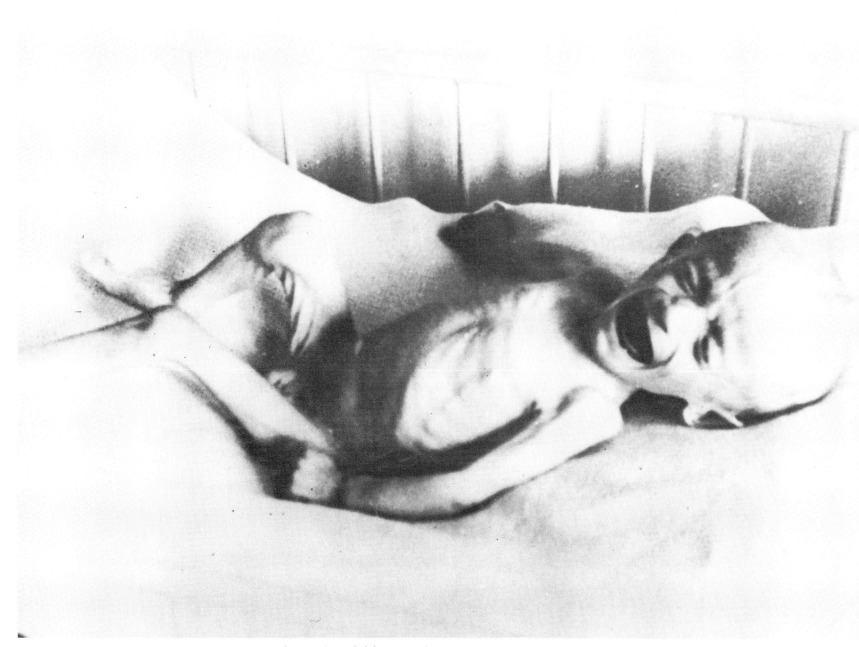

A starving child is found at Belsen, barely alive, by British troops after the liberation.

She was amused by Belsen horror camp
film. This German woman was one of the
civilians in the village of Burgsetinfurt
who were ordered by military government authorities to view documentary
motion pictures showing the actual
horrors of the Belsen and Buchenwald
camps. On leaving the theatre after the
showing, she laughed. Here, she is
being ordered to return and view the
film again. Captain A. Stirling, the acting
district assistant provost marshal,
motions the callous woman back into
the theatre.

Liberated occupants of the camp at Belsen are taking showers in the open air baths set up by the British who captured the camp.

Nordhausen, Germany. Brutal Nazi crime was uncovered at the Nordhausen-Lager concentration camp by soldiers of the Third Armored Division. Corpses here await burial by the American Army, using German civilian labor. The bodies of hundreds of slave laborers of many nationalities were found in conditions almost unrecognizable as human. The dead lay beside the sick and dying in the same beds. Most were dead when the camp was taken. The survivors were all removed to hospitals.

An open mass grave of slave laborers
at Nordhausen.

Rows of bodies of dead inmates fill the yard at Nordhausen Gestapo concentration camp. Photo shows less than half of the bodies dead of starvation and shooting at the hands of Gestapo men. The almost 4,000 inmates were French, Polish, Belgian, Russian and several German political prisoners.

A dying victim at Nordhausen. Too weak to sit up amid the rags and filth, he gazes up at his American soldier liberators. Only 500 were left by the time the Americans overran the camp.

Nordhausen, 1945. Germans removing
dead political prisoners to be buried,
as American troops supervise.

On order of the military government the buergemeister of Nordhausen got 600 men to dig graves for the 2,500 political prisoners who died in the camp, all of whom were unburied. The men were then sent to the camp to carry the bodies to the graves for burial. Here, the Germans placing a body in the grave.

The pathetic scene of a young Polish boy whose grandmother was a torture victim of the Nazis at Nordhausen. The boy steadfastly refused to allow Germans to bury his kin. Grim-faced American G.I.'s look on in quiet sympathy.

German atrocities in Holland. The ill-famed German concentration camp in Vught near Hertogenbosch. Undeniable evidence of torturing and murder of Dutch patriots was found everywhere in this hell where 13,000 people were killed. One of the cremation furnaces is pictured here.

The remains of the gallows at Vught, found by the Allied troops, from which the victims were hanged.

Blocks upon which victims were made to stand when being hanged. It can be seen that the feet of the victim were hardly far enough from the ground to come even close to breaking a neck when blocks were knocked from underneath.

177

More than 300 bodies roasted in a barn just outside Gardelegen, were still smoldering when General Simpson of the 9th Army took the town. Slave laborers were herded into the barn with gasoline-soaked straw. When the fear-crazed men tried to break out of the blazing barn, they were ruthlessly machine-gunned down. Here are some of the bodies outside who mangaed to get through only to be shot. G.I.'s observe the dead in silence and disgust.

American soldiers stand by while German civilians are forced to uncover the bodies of 700 victims of Nazi brutality in the Gardelegen concentration camp. The bodies of hundreds of slave laborers who had been massacred, some burned alive by the Germans, were found by American soldiers who captured the camp. German citizens were forced to dig graves to provide for decent burial.

Bodies of Poles and Russians lie where they were shot by S.S. guards in the concentration camp at Ohrdurf, Germany. For lack of transportation, these men could not be moved by Nazis before U.S. Third Army occupied the town, so they were executed by order of the camp commandant.

Supreme Commander of Allied Forces Europe, General Dwight D. Eisenhower and a party of high ranking officers including General George Patton (standing behind Ike) and General Omar Bradley (four stars on helmet), view dead bodies of war prisoners shot by Nazis at Ohrdurf, Germany, after the Allied forces had captured the camp.

Bodies of Jewish prisoners at Landsberg camp are observed by a U.S. Brigadier General after the camp had been liberated by Twelfth Armored Division troops.

The commandant of Landsberg concentration camp stands amid some of the victims who died at his hand.

Rapid advancing units of Patch's Seventh U.S. Army overran another horror camp at Landsberg, west of Munich. Once again ghastly scenes of Nazi brutality were prominent. Over 4,000 Jews of every nationality were burnt alive by their S.S. guards when the camp was threatened by the Twelfth U.S. Armored division. Some of the prisoners managed to crawl out of their blazing huts and were quickly shot. Others were burnt alive—too weak to move.

Photo shows two German civilians carrying the body of one of the victims murdered by S.S. guards at Landsberg. Two hundred German civilians were rounded up and forced to dig graves, after they had been conducted on a tour of the camp, and seen for themselves some of the ghastly atrocities committed by their fellow Germans.

Harsh wooden shoes worn by slave laborers at the Penig concentration camp. All the women airplane workers had to walk miles to and from the factory where they assembled plane parts.

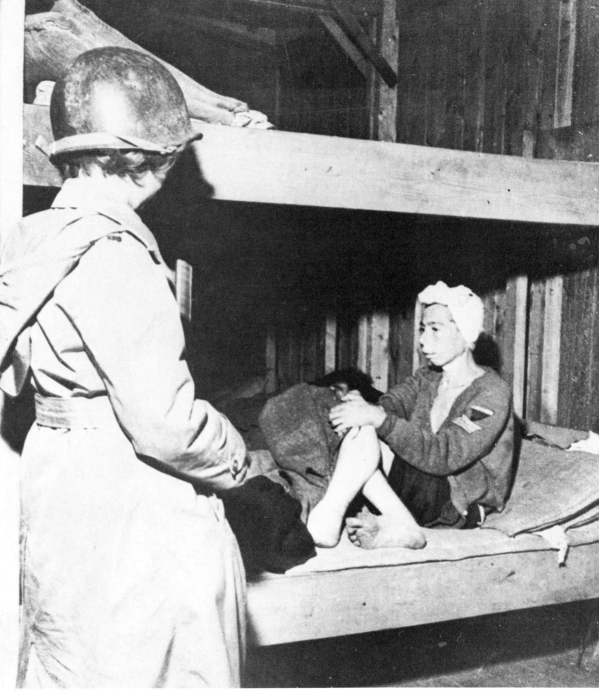

Photo shows U.S. Army nurse approaching emaciated Jewish girl in her miserable straw and sacking bed. "Corpses still alive and walking around!" was how this picture was described by a U.S. Army photographer. This girl was one of 68 Jewish women from Budapest starved and forced to work in a Luftwaffe airplane factory. This is in the camp at Penig.

Gotha, Germany. Felled by malnutrition, disease and Nazi brutality, these prisoners' bodies are piled like cordwood in a corner of the death camp. Major John Scotti of Brooklyn, N.Y., surveys the evidence of Nazi madness.

Charred bodies of prisoners at Gotha concentration camp are observed by Supreme Allied Commander General Dwight D. Eisenhower and a party of high ranking officers including Gen. Omar Bradley (foreground, next to Eisenhower, fourth from left) and Gen. George S. Patton (fourth right from Bradley, with pearl handled sidearm).

Gotha, Germany. When Gen. George S. Patton's Fourth Armored Division overran the Nazi concentration camp south of Gotha, many unburned bodies were found. Internees at this camp were Poles, Czechs, German Jews and German political prisoners. They were forced to labor at nearby installations. In a woodshed at the back of the camp were many naked bodies stacked like logs. Many bore marks of vicious floggings. Lime had been sprinkled over them to prevent odor and the spread of disease.

Lublin murder camp. When the Red
Army approached Lublin, the Germans
hastily exhumed previously buried bodies
for burning. However they did not
have the time.

Lublin Murder Camp. One of the storehouses for clothing taken from the victims. This one contained over one million pairs of shoes.

Lublin murder camp. One of the incinera-
tors that disposed of the bodies,
observed by German citizens after the
camp was liberated.

The Lublin camp of annihilation. On August 11, 1944, Konstantin Simonov, well-known Russian poet and dramatist, published the first part of his account of the Lublin concentration camp, known among the Germans as the "camp of annihilation," where thousands of men and women of all nationalities, Poles, Russians, Ukraines as well as thousands of Jews, were tortured and killed. Built over an area of twenty-five square kilometers, the camp was not intended to provide permanent accommodation for the inmates, and the barracks were cleared just as fast as the prisoners could be killed. Some of them died of hunger and disease, but the favorite method was by gas. The bodies were cremated in huge ovens. This picture shows cans of cyclon B. poison gas with which the prisoners were killed after being packed into ferro-concrete cells built all over the camp.

Struthof concentration camp. Guard
posts are high and not too far apart.
Note elaborate double fence system.
Natzviller area, France.

At the Struthof concentration camp, Natzviller area, France. Food for the prisoners consisted of no more than pitiful chopped potato tops. Demonstrated here by a Free French intelligence guide for an American soldier.

Struthof concentration camp. Before
bodies were stored away for later
cremation, many bodies were brought to
this room and autopsies were performed to test effects of the war gas
used on victims.

Military government personnel of 69th Infantry Division, U.S. Seventh Army, look for identification on bodies of victims of German atrocities, discovered in mass graves in a sand pit east of Zeitz, Germany. Bodies of approximately 400 victims were found. The victims were inmates of a nearby concentration camp named Brabag. Bodies were buried two months before arrival of U.S. tank columns, according to civilians.

Terror camp in Holland. Two British
soldiers examine one of the three ovens
used for cremation of victims in concentration camp at Herlogenbosch,
Holland.

A Pole, formerly an inmate at the Ludwigslust concentration camp liberated by the 82nd Airborne Division, drops dead from malnutrition. Polish woman also freed from the camp passes by carrying shoes confiscated from local German women. The American 82nd Airborne and the British Second Army found the bodies of hundreds of dead prisoners at the concentration camp near Ludwigslust, formerly operated by the Nazi party and S.S. troops. Bodies of Polish, German, Russian, French, Dutch and Belgian prisoners and forced laborers were found in one building, and bodies of victims of Nazi torture were found heaped in pits in a yard, one pit containing 300 bodies. Victims had died from persistent torture and starvation, and many bodies showed evidence of strangulation and fatal floggings.

Sprawling grotesquely in the prison enclosure are the burnt bodies of slave laborers and Jews burnt alive by their Nazi guards.

Russian slave workers liberated by the British Army from a camp near Osnabruck, were in the act of recovering clothing from the basement of a store in the town. A German policeman, allowed by the military government to continue his duties discovered them in the act and waiting until a considerable number of them had descended into the basement, set fire to it. Many of the Russians were trapped below and overcome by smoke and fumes from the burning clothing. The British Army photographer who took this picture, being first on the scene, immediately dispatched his driver for military assistance which quickly arrived and began the work of the rescue. Many of the Russians had to be given artificial respiration but, despite tremendous efforts made to save them, two Russian women collapsed and died. April, 1945.

199

S.S. troops massacred a whole French village. On June 10, 1944, a report was issued on the massacre of Oradour-sur-Galne, a village about sixteen miles from Limoges, one of the most barbarous atrocities on the list of crimes perpetrated by the Germans in France. Of over 750 inhabitants of Oradour-sur-Galne, only *seven* escaped the German butchers. Men were rounded up, pushed into a nearby barn and shot on the spot. After the men had been massacred, the women and the children were taken inside the village and burned alive. Other S.S. in the meantime went through the village drenching the houses with an incendiary product and then set them ablaze till they burned to ashes. Pictured, French men, women and children, shot and/or burned to death, barely recognizable as human forms.

Besarabia. Men waiting to be shot by Nazis.

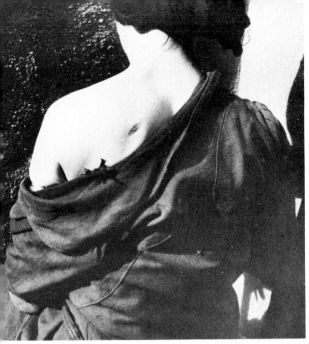

No. 3 work camp at Erla near Leipzig, where the Nazis evacuated the slave laborers except for about 100 who were too weak to be moved. These were put into building which was set afire. Only two Poles escaped and told the American troops of the incident. One sits next to a dead friend and bows his head in grief.

Distomo, Greece. Among the many cruelties discovered in Greek villages after the rout of the Nazis in Greece was this. The woman is Zoi Secremeli of the village of Distomo, where many inhabitants were slaughtered by Nazi troops. This woman was nursing her nine-month-old child when a bullet crashed through the child's head and into Zoi's body where it emerged from her shoulder. She shows the scar she will always bear.

Thirty-four flag-draped caskets are laid out in the snow in Bande, Belgium, just before the funeral procession and the burial of thirty-four young men between the ages of seventeen and twenty-one who were shot down by the Nazis during the re-occupation of this town. According to British official statement the young men were forced into a labor battalion and when they completed their work they were herded into a cellar and then one by one compelled to pass through a doorway. As they entered they were shot in the back by Nazis standing behind the door. The bodies were recovered and prepared for burial after the Allies re-entered the town.

Looking through the barbed wire are a
few of the 1,000 Russian, Serb, Italian,
Polish and French prisoners who were
held by the Nazis in this camp at
Sarreguemines, France. Some of them
had been captives of the Nazis since
1939. The camp was captured by
General George S. Patton's Third Army,
which had advanced so fast that the
Germans had no time to transfer the
captives. Date of photo, December 1944.

Returned escaped prisoners are overcome with joy at finding friends still alive
at the infamous Erla camp.

The double hanging of two Polish
civilians in public on a Warsaw street.
The murders followed a round-up of
Polish citizens by the Nazis.

An electrified high voltage fence which
surrounded a Nazi slave labor camp
found in the Vosges mountains of France.

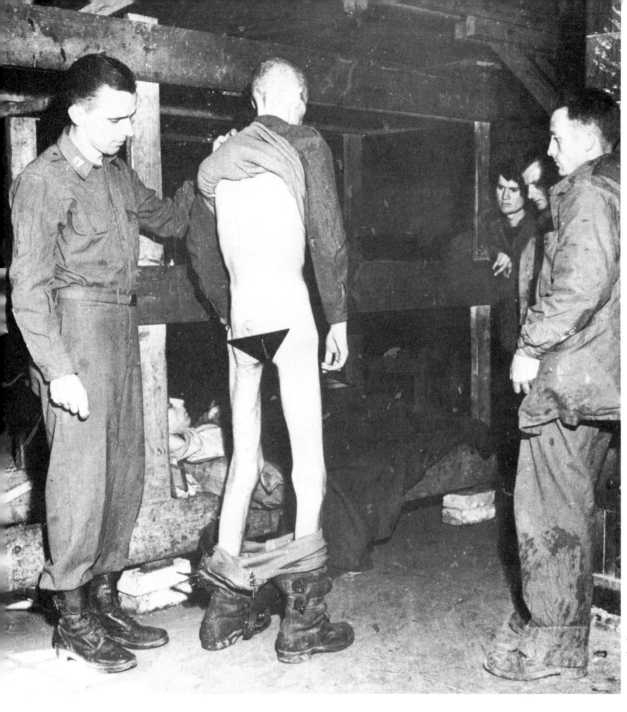

An American war prisoner in Germany
who was liberated when U.S. forces
overran the territory surrounding the
camp, displays his horribly wasted body
with his spine protruding through
his skin.

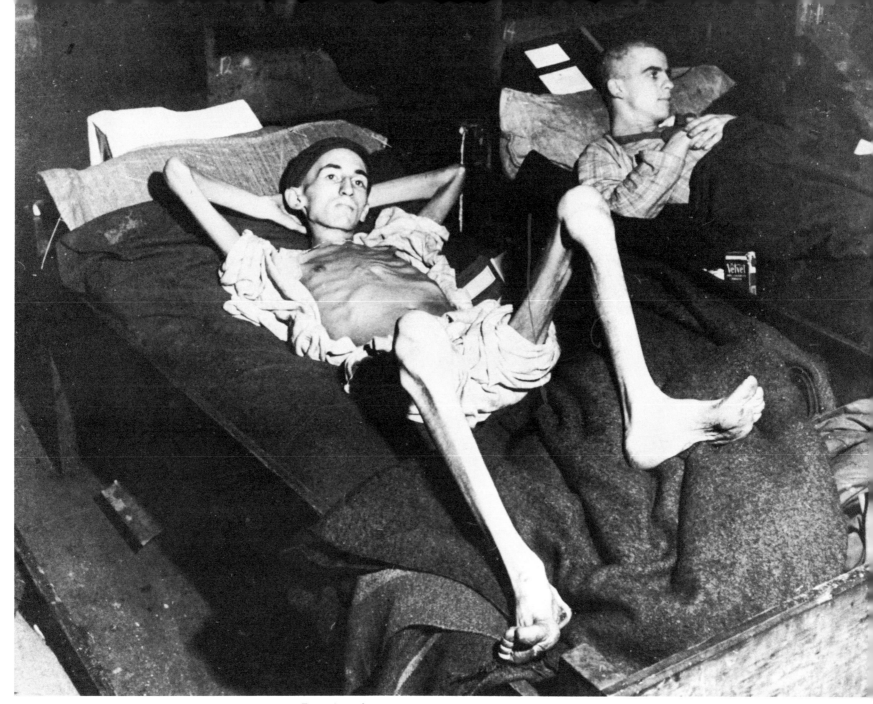

Emaciated Americans freed from a
P.O.W. camp in Germany.

As the Nazis withdrew from the city of Kerch at the start of the Russian winter offensives, they killed as many of the civilians as they could including many women and children. Picture shows mothers and children shot by the Nazi troops.

Naples, Italy. The horrible playfulness of Nazi soldiers, so hardened by super-race teachings that pain and death were matters for laughter, was responsible for the senseless maiming of these two Italian boys. They are Guido Brandi, thirteen, who lost both his legs, and his brother Thomaso, sixteen, (nearest the camera) who lost one leg. During the German occupation of Naples the boys were working in a field with their parents, close to a building occupied by Nazis as a headquarters. Two Nazi soldiers who worked in the building appeared at a window and beckoned the boys to them. Suspecting nothing, they approached. When they were about fifteen yards away one of the German soldiers threw something to them—the boys thought it was a present and tried to catch it——it was a present all right——a real Nazi present: a live hand grenade. It burst between them. Guido fell immediately with both legs shattered. Thomaso managed to run about 50 yards towards his parents before collapsing. The Nazis, after watching the grenade explode, disappeared. Photo date, March 1945.

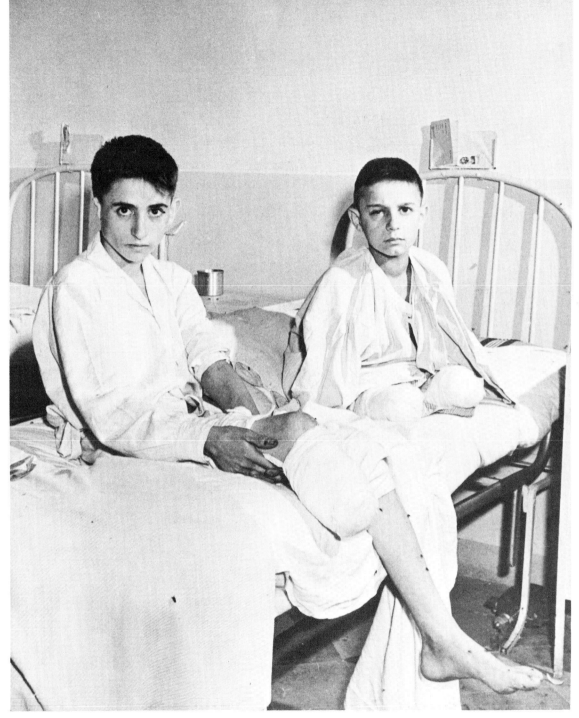

Another photo of dead Polish Jews in Warsaw, shown awaiting the death cart on its daily visit. Even Christian Poles were forbidden meat and milk.

Tattooed by Nazis. These girls were Jewish slave workers taken to the camp liberated by the U.S. Ninth Army. They were forced to work in German munitions factories. They came from Italy, France, Holland, Belgium, Poland, Czechoslovakia, etc. Each had a yellow cross painted on the back, and all, even the children were tattooed on the left arm with their identification number.

German civilians are forced to view the atrocities committed by their fellow Germans in Czechoslovakia. Here, they file past the bodies of 30 Jewish women starved to death by S.S. troops in a 300-mile march across Czechoslovakia. Buried in shallow graves near the town of Volary, the bodies were exhumed by German citizens under direction of U.S. Army medics of the 5th Infantry, U.S. Third Army, in May 1945.

In many countries of the world before World War II there were many thousands, perhaps millions, of people whose views on Adolf Hitler of Germany and Benito Mussolini of Italy ranged from general approval to outright support. In France, admiration for Hitler in high places did as much to undermine that country's capacity to wage war successfully as did outdated military concepts and political disunity. In England, public support for the Nazi regime came from Sir Oswald Mosley's British Union of Fascists; from many prominent people such as Lord Redesdale; from the Imperial Fascist League led by Arnold Leese, and from the National Socialist League founded by John Becket and by William Joyce, who subsequently became notorious as Lord Haw-Haw for his wartime propaganda broadcasts from Germany. Even the Prince of Wales, later King Edward VIII, still later the Duke of Windsor, appeared to admire some aspects of Nazism.

In the U.S.A. there were a number of advocates of doctrines which included Fascists, anti-Semites, anti-Communists and pro-Germans. These advocates were often confused, and came in all ideological guises. They shared, however, the belief that the U.S.A. was dominated by those they considered degenerates and traitors; they consistently blamed the Jews and often the Negroes, and professed great admiration for the philosophy of Nazism. Some were cranks and psychopaths. Many were well-financed and well-educated.

The brown-shirted storm troopers of the German-American Bund, with their Nazi salutes and their swastika flags, had for some years before World War II become a familiar sight in many cities of the East and the Middle West. They were mostly first- and second-generation Americans of German origin, but included others. Their leader, Fritz Kuhn, had drawn an enthusiastic crowd of 22,000 to a rally at Madison Square Garden in 1939; and by that year, the Bund had organized 22 youth camps located near military centers. Kuhn was convicted later that year for embezzling Bund funds, and the movement collapsed; but until then the German government, while refusing publicly to approve of the Bund, had been supporting the movement in private.

There was Father Charles E. Coughlin, the widely known "radio priest" of Michigan, who had long been a bitter critic of Franklin Delano Roosevelt. He had been disciplined by the Catholic hierarchy after his vicious efforts in the 1936 election, but by 1940 he was back again in the public forum. He had established a weekly newspaper called *Social Justice* with a circulation of 185,000 copies. He made no secret of his anti-Semitism and of his admiration for Hitler. In 1942 he wrote that Germany was the victim of a "sacred war" instigated by "the race of Jews" and that England and America were obeying banker-politicians who were their Jewish masters. This was identical to the line being used at that time by Goebbels in his Nazi propaganda. Father Coughlin had a large nationwide following among those who were against the New Deal, and among Irish Catholics who, for historical reasons, had a strong anti-British bias.

Some pro-Nazi groups were faintly absurd. There was, for instance, a militant feminist group called "We, The Mothers Mobilize for America, Inc." They distinguished themselves by demanding that the U.S. Army send troops to the Mexican border to repel an invasion by 200,000 "Communist Jews;" an invasion which existed only in their fevered imaginations. In 1942 they instigated a campaign to impeach President Roosevelt for having arranged the attack on Pearl Harbor with the Japanese.

"We, the Mothers Mobilize for America, Inc." was led by such women as Mrs. Agnes Waters, Mrs. Lyrl Van Hyning and Mrs. Elizabeth Dilling, who proclaimed with a stridency which hid a shortage of facts, that America was fighting the wrong enemy. That enemy was the Communist Underground among whom, according to Mrs. Dilling, was Eleanor Roosevelt, the President's wife.

While in retrospect it seems remarkable that "We, the Mothers Mobilize for America, Inc." could have been taken seriously, they were nevertheless well organized in many cities, mobilized marches, and produced floods of newsletters and leaflets.

Father Coughlin was not the only minister of religion to show public support for Nazi philosophy. Another was the Rev. Gerald B. Winrod who organized the "Defenders of the Christian Faith" in Kansas. A third was the Rev. Gerald L. K. Smith, a Southern evangelist who had helped Senator Huey Pierce Long deceive the gullible with his "Share the Wealth" slogan.

In 1940, the Rev. Smith formed his "Committee of One Million." His magazine, *Cross and the Flag,* regularly denounced the President for supporting world communism.

Other anti-Semitic and pro-Nazi organizations included "The Knights of the White Camelia" lead by George Deatherage; "The Black Legion," "The Sentinels of the Republic," "The American Vigilant Intelligence Federation," and "The Christian Front."

The most sophisticated of the Fascists was probably Lawrence Dennis. Educated at Harvard, Dennis was the proprietor of the "Weekly Foreign Letter" which claimed to to give well-informed "inside" intelligence on what was really happening abroad. He was an editor at *Reader's Digest*. Most of it was in favor of Germany and Italy.

On the West Coast, an organization called "The Friends of Progress" was led by Robert Noble and Ellis O. Jones. It denounced the American government for its war against Germany and Japan and accused General MacArthur as a deserter who had abandoned his troops at Manila.

The oddest of the Fascists was William Dudley Pelley. He fancied himself to be, among other things, a Nazi gauleiter. He also played the role of the mystic. He said that he had died in 1926 but had been restored to life, and that during his brief visit to heaven had made the acquaintance of an "oracle" who now guided all his activities.

When Hitler came to power in 1933 Pelley's "oracle" had directed him to become America's Hitler and to organize "The Silver Shirt Legion." From then on, he worked intensively to obtain followers for his strange mixture of metaphysics and politics. The slogan for his crusade was "For Christ and the Constitution," and in his magazine *The Galilean,* described as "the magazine of Aquarian Soulcraft" he propounded a kind of Nazi theology. To Pelley, democracy was a Jewish invention, and he echoed Hitler's view of the Volk as being the aristocratic principle of nature. In an article headed "The Coming World Axis," he prophesied a new world order commanded from Berlin and the "cremation" of "the putrid corpse of Jewish democracy."

Pelley, and many others, may well now be dismissed as crackpots. Yet, they had between them a very considerable following, and there was a consistent pattern underlying their apparently confused and confusing doctrines. Their demagoguery was consistent in its intense hatred for Jews, and liberals, who were equated with Communists; its opposition to democracy, and its admiration for Nazi discipline. Strictly, a Nazi was a member of the German Nazi Party, and so none of these people or their admirers was a Nazi in the technical sense. But they were Nazis in spirit, as were many of the "respectable" American businessmen who sympathized with them and often supported those and similar movements with considerable sums of money.

Some of those men, early admirers of Hitler, such as Charles Lindbergh in the U.S. and Lord Redesdale in England, changed to serve their countries with patriotism and integrity when war came. Nonetheless, they all demonstrated that Nazism was not, and is not, a purely Hitlerite or German attitude of mind. It exists everywhere, in all countries, even today; a principle of evil which is never, even in the most favorable circumstances, far from the surface.

Charles Coughlin was a Catholic priest who hated Franklin Roosevelt and the New Deal with such intensity that Hitler and the Nazis were heroic people to him. He adopted Hitler's anti-Jewish theme and his national newspaper, *Social Justice* was full of praise and sympathy for the Nazi struggle against the Jews and the communists. He drew as many as 18,000 people to his rallies. He was finally silenced by his Church superiors.

Charles Lindbergh was an American folk hero turned sour. He visited Germany, met with Hitler, accepted a decoration from the Nazis.

He was an important national influence in gaining sympathy for the Nazis in their "anti-communist struggle" against the "international money-lenders." As the times heated up, he became more open in his anti-Semitism.

In recent years attempts have been made to whitewash and distort what he did. The fact is that he was a very effective propaganda agent for the Nazis.

John Edgar Hoover ran a very peculiar Federal Bureau of Investigation. He ignored organized crime, thus allowing it to flourish and grow. He was so fanatical about "the menace of communism" that he made anti-communism rather than anti-crime the top priority at the FBI.

Hoover openly admired the "discipline" of the Nazi regime. Until the day war broke out between the U.S. and Germany he continued to cooperate with the Nazi secret police, helping them to identify and locate "pro-communists" who were often tortured and killed.

Joseph P. Kennedy hated communists, liberals and Jews. He despised blacks. As Ambassador to Great Britain he was so pro-Hitler that President Franklin Roosevelt was forced to recall him in 1941. When his son ran for the Presidency in 1960, his strategy was to completely disassociate himself from his father's history and political views.

Like their father, Robert and John Kennedy were supporters of Senator Joseph McCarthy. This too was successfully buried in the campaign that elected the son of Nazi-sympathizer Kennedy to the highest office in the land.

Lawrence Dennis was a big fan of Hitler and the Nazis. Serving as an editor of Reader's Digest he simultaneously consorted with top American native fascists, many of whom were indicted, along with Dennis, in 1944. The charge: conspiracy to overthrow the Government of the United States.

In this photo, Dennis stands with Baron Ulrich Von Guinanth. The two were attending a Nazi party conference in Nuremberg in 1937. The Baron was later identified as the Nazi pay-off man in the United States and interned in West Virginia.

During most of this period, Dennis remained on the payroll of the Reader's Digest.

EPILOGUE

In the preceding pages some of the atrocities committed by the Nazis have been shown; but for every picture, for every recorded incident, there were thousands of persecutions, cruelties and tortures, whose only record remains in the memories of the victims or their survivors.

There is, in all human beings, the capacity for cruelty. Perhaps one definition of a civilized community is one in which this dark urge is balanced and held in check by philosophies, religious beliefs and institutions committed to higher aspirations and to humane concerns. History has demonstrated that this balance is precarious. Disagreement with particular views can become the kind of intolerance which in turn can lead to political action which, if not held within reasonable bounds, can result in authoritarianism and tyranny. The best chance of containing such growths lies in the plural and democratic societies.

These are by no means necessarily the most "efficient" societies in the short term, but they provide the only protection we know against the one efficiency which can be guaranteed by totalitarianism, whether of the Right or of the Left—that is, the efficiency of tyranny.

It would be pleasant to be able to record that in the years since World War II the number of plural and democratic societies has been increasing. Unfortunately, the contrary is the case. Authoritarianism is on the increase. Even the Nazi aspirations, its racialism, its intense intolerance, its hungry power urges are on the increase. Nor, in spite of disastrous experience, has Nazism itself died. In Germany the neo-Nazis still try to spread their poison. There is a Nazi party here in America. In England, although Sir Oswald Mosley's Fascists no longer exist as a group, the same attitude finds expression under a different name. These neo-Nazis are, at present, tiny groups, sometimes laughable, existing on the fringes of their societies and without significant influence. But the same could have been said of the Nazi Party when it first took shape in the Germany of 1919 in the smoky room of a cheap tavern in Munich. It was born out of a small group founded by a railway mechanic by the name of Anton Drexler, called the German Workers' Party, which included a few insignificant nationalists and anti-Semites.

To what extent do we learn from history? The answer, alas, appears to be very little, for each succeeding generation seems prone to the same, everlasting mistakes of the one before. One is tempted to wonder whether, a generation or two from now, there will not be another such picture gallery as this one, depicting new men and new atrocities under a different name at a different time.

INDEX